With best wishes.

W.K. McSlimmings.

January 1977.

THOMSON McLINTOCK & CO – THE FIRST HUNDRED YEARS

Mr Thomson McLintock

THOMSON McLINTOCK & CO – THE FIRST HUNDRED YEARS

REX WINSBURY

Produced by
Seeley, Service & Co. Ltd
196 Shaftesbury Avenue, London WC2H 8JL

ISBN *0 85422 136 0*

This book is intended solely for distribution to past and present partners and staff of Thomson McLintock & Co and of McLintock Main Lafrentz & Co, to these firms' clients and to friends in the business professions.

Printed in Great Britain
by Ebenezer Baylis and Son, Ltd
The Trinity Press, Worcester, and London

CONTENTS

ILLUSTRATIONS

Foreword

THIS BOOK is dedicated to the late Mr Thomson McLintock JP CA ACA and to all those who subsequently joined him and succeeded him to pioneer the development of the offices of Thomson McLintock & Co in which the present partners of the firm are proud to serve.

The author, Mr Rex Winsbury, a senior member of staff of *The Financial Times*, London, kindly undertook to take possession of all the research material already amassed and collated by Professor and Mrs TE James (old friends and clients of the Glasgow office) and to carry out whatever further inquiries he felt were necessary. He had been asked to 'look in at our window' and write frankly about us, past, present and future 'just as he saw us', and this he has done. It is hoped that those who read this book will find interest in it and derive a little entertainment from it. The purpose of publishing the history of Thomson McLintock & Co 1877–1977 is to create a lasting record and impression of its first hundred years for all who are presently or may in the future be connected with it. On behalf of all the partners I thank Mr Winsbury for his completed work. All those partners, retired partners and friends with whom he has talked have enjoyed his penetrating and analytical questioning. He has, on page xi, acknowledged the many sources on which he has drawn in writing this book. I know he will not mind my adding to his words of thanks the gratitude of the partners to Professor and Mrs TE James for their homeric work in digging into the past and producing so much information which, but for their efforts, would have been lost in the mists of time.

I invite you to open these pages and I trust that you will find sufficient in them to provide you with both interest and pleasure.

Chairman Centenary Committee
216 West George Street, Glasgow

Acknowledgments

FIRST AND foremost, I must thank Professor and Mrs TE James for the detailed, thorough and illuminating research work which they carried out into the earlier years of Thomson McLintock & Co. Without that work, this book would not have been possible, and I have drawn freely and copiously upon their findings. I must also thank numerous partners in the firm for their unstinting time and help, in particular (but in no particular order) Sir William Slimmings, Mr John Kirkpatrick, Mr Alan McLintock, Mr James Macnair, Mr Donald Ironside, Mr David Parkes, Mr Harry Pritchard, Mr Bill Morrison, Mr George Caldwell, Mr Blair Smith. Two retired partners, Mr Leslie Bell and Mr Tom Currie, have also given me invaluable help in tracing the development of the firm, while to Mr LeRoy Layton I owe valuable insights into the dynamics of the international firm of McLintock Main Lafrentz. Mr John Owen has displayed the patience and determination of an ex-Marine in coping with the organizational side of this book, while to Mrs Debbie Scholfield goes the credit for the smooth running of the day-to-day operation. Lastly, my thanks and commiserations to the efficient girls who have had to type and retype the drafts of this book at the McLintock London office.

RW

Introduction

A FIRM of accountants, unlike a manufacturing company, has no physical assets; its only assets are its people. Unlike a financial company, it has no reserves, except its reserves of skill, experience and probity. Unlike a trading company, it has no patent rights, brand names or sales messages; it cannot advertise, and its only selling point is its reputation. The story of an accountancy firm is therefore bound to be a highly personal one, about the men (and latterly the women) who founded and guided the firm, and staff it. The story of Thomson McLintock & Co is, however, more personal than most; it is by any standard, inside or outside the accountancy profession, an intensely personal firm. Its partners say that it is, believe that it is, and try to ensure that it remains so.

Here then we must look for the real justification for telling the Thomson McLintock story on the occasion of its centenary. A centenary is a conventional but, it must be admitted, often arbitrary excuse for looking back over 100 years. But in the case of Thomson McLintock & Co, the firm has for the past fifteen years or so been undergoing a period of rapid change and expansion, through which the partners and managers have been endeavouring to preserve the personal spirit that has characterized the firm, that has been the main reason why many of them joined it in the first place and stayed with it, and indeed has exerted a decisive influence on the manner in which the firm has changed and expanded, within the UK and outside it, in response to the business pressures of the 1960s and 1970s.

For in grappling—rather belatedly, as McLintock men will be the first to admit—with the problem of providing not only a nation-wide service to major clients, but also in extending that service to all the major industrial and developing countries, McLintocks has adopted, partly by necessity and partly by choice, a distinctive federalist approach which leaves substantial autonomy in the hands of local partners, while seeking to promote common standards and techniques by means of general consensus. It is fair to say that, entering late into the international game, as into the national one, the cost of a different approach—the cost of opening up new branches and developing new business—would in any case have been prohibitive.

But, because of its basic philosophy, its prizing of the individual and his right to his opinion, McLintocks had an answer to this problem, and therefore attracted into its national federation, and into the international federation of McLintock Main Lafrentz, firms in the major cities of Great Britain and of the world which are of essentially like mind—individualists who value their own freedoms and powers of decision, and have seen the advantage in joining such a federation without having to submerge their individual identities.

TMcL—to use the firm's own favoured abbreviation—is therefore carrying out, in keeping with its own individual character, a highly individual experiment in organization, with a new organization structure recently introduced for both the national and the international firms, the essence of which is that each part of the federation contributes, in ideas and personnel, to the reaching of the final decisions. Like all such structures, it will no doubt be modified with experience, and it makes great calls upon the time of those who operate it; but it fits the character of the firm.

Now one of the eight largest accountancy firms of Great Britain, TMcL began 100 years ago as a family business in Glasgow. It is therefore neither the oldest nor the largest of UK accountants, but it has at least as great a commitment to the profession as any other firm, through its involvement with the accountants' institutes, in particular the Scottish Institute.

The very idea of a formal body of accountants emanated from the founder of the Edinburgh firm that is now part of the McLintock federation, and TMcL has produced more presidents of The Institute of Chartered Accountants of Scotland than any other single firm. To this list there should shortly be added by happy coincidence John Kirkpatrick, joint senior partner in Glasgow, who is currently vice-president and thereby president-designate of the Institute, in line to hold that office during McLintocks' centenary year of 1977.

This involvement reflects the professionalism and tradition of personal service that have characterized the firm from the beginning, and which it tries to foster and preserve, by, for example, ensuring that all clients have access to partners, even if this means a higher ratio than usual of partners to staff. In this sense, over the hundred years, the firm has stuck to the qualities of its founder, the original Mr Thomson McLintock of Glasgow. But the problem that has confronted his successors in the 1960s and 1970s has been the problem of size. As in so many industries, a firm must be of a certain size to support the necessary central services that clients now demand (for example, expertise in computer auditing, in which McLintocks is strong); but at the same time there was a real reluctance to get too big too fast, for fear of sacrificing the basic qualities of the firm.

McLintocks' ranking in the UK—not one of the Big Four firms, but somewhere in the next four, depending on how it is measured—has therefore in one sense been deliberate, and in another sense has defined the business challenge confronting its partners, as they sought to provide a full range of services, to the full geographical extent, without damaging the traditions of the firm as they felt and still feel them.

Not surprisingly, a firm which has grown up in this sort of way, with this sort of people, has from time to time had its internal differences of opinion. Expansion to London in the period of the first world war and after brought differences between the firm's founder and his most talented son; under that son, the London office flourished and eventually split off from the parent office in Glasgow, only to be reunited in 1959; in its turn, the London office probably neglected opportunities for expansion between the wars which left McLintocks' post-war partners with the problem of catching up on their bigger competitors; when the decision to 'go international' was taken, not everyone agreed with it. No doubt there will be more such disagreements; in a firm of this type, it would be unnatural for such disagreements not to arise and be expressed, for many of its constituent firms and partners are in it precisely because it is a place where opposing views can be aired and listened to. The art of the managerial system adopted by McLintocks is to reconcile this freedom with the need for common policies and standards, on lines which in the end are accepted by all.

In this reconciliation, it has certainly helped that the firm has always had at its head one or two 'strong men'. Indeed, there is still running through the firm a certain sense of paternalism that derives from the Glasgow office and its very Scottish, almost puritan, character that persisted until very recently. If 'paternalism' is these days regarded as a somewhat old-fashioned attribute, it is none the worse for that. The presence of 'strong men' at the top has helped to ensure that discussion and disagreement have finally been reconciled in a decision that is generally accepted; in a sense, the existence of these 'wise men' at the top has been the necessary counter-weight to the loose federal structure underneath.

These men—and one may mention Sir William McLintock, creator of the London office; Sir John Morison, senior partner in London in the 1950s; James Dowling, for twenty years the best-known accountant in Scotland and senior partner in Scotland for ten years—have been a great asset to the firm in their own right, and this tradition is carried on by men such as Sir William Slimmings, the present senior partner in London. Such figures are big getters of business, and are in their way standard-bearers for the firm as a whole.

Partners in McLintocks seldom take on outside directorships; the firm's policy is not to take such positions as a routine part of business, but only to take certain institutional board posts. The firm neither is, nor has sought to be, a virtual household name in the way that some of its big league competitors are—relying more on its reputation among, say, the big banks and government for work than on a glamorous public image (one may almost visualize certain partners of McLintocks curling up at the very idea of a glamorous image). The obverse of this is that McLintocks has kept well clear of what may be called the 'fringes' of the tax avoidance business.

At the back of these distinctive features of the firm (and of course one should not claim them to be unique) lies the solid bread-and-butter work of the accountant, the audit. Thomson McLintock & Co is in the end a 'general practitioner'; it has a strong tax side, a national spread, an international capability, precisely because all large accountancy practices have these days to offer these facilities to clients, or at least to the larger clients. There is a strong defensive element here—accountants who cannot offer this range of services are apt to see their best clients vanishing elsewhere. The tax side is also a big breeder of audit work. At one time, between the wars, the firm was involved in a lot of amalgamation work—indeed, it was involved in the series of mergers that created one of the UK's largest international companies, ICI; it is still joint auditor of ICI to this day. While this type of work has dropped off proportionately, a great deal of 'man in the middle' work still gets done, especially in Scotland, and there is plenty of 'spin off' work from situations that the firm still gets called in from time to time to sort out.

A strong involvement in London with the shipping industry and the shipping 'conferences', and a long history of trade association work dating back to the 1920s, have also proved fruitful sources of fees and contacts. Some offices are strong in local authority work; other offices have a big stake in shipbuilding work. But the backbone of the business is still the basic auditing function, especially that done for the big clients, among whom are ICI, the National Coal Board, the Co-operative Wholesale Society, Associated British Foods, Leicester Building Society, large sections of the whisky industry (naturally) and of the shipbuilding industry, Grand Metropolitan, and many other prestigious names. Grand Met in particular has a unique place in the annals of Thomson McLintock & Co. For it was the realization that the Grand Met connection, which TMcL had seen grow from small beginnings, would be at risk if McLintocks could not follow the big hotel group's expansion overseas and cope with its auditing needs outside the United Kingdom, that finally convinced the sceptics in the firm that it had to 'go international'.

This is not to imply that the firm had until the 1960s no interests outside Glasgow and London; there were Manchester and Birmingham offices long before that, and there was the curious episode of the Paris office opened briefly in the early 1930s and shut again in a manner which suggested almost that Paris did not have quite the right moral tone for a branch of a puritan Scottish accountancy firm (Paris now has a strong McLintock Main Lafrentz office). There was also the Lisbon office, opened for the express reason of serving that very glamorous (perhaps McLintocks' most glamorous) client, Calouste Gulbenkian. But these forays outside the Glasgow-London axis were just that—forays, rather than a systematic battle plan. Put another way, the corporate shape of Thomson McLintock & Co in England as it found itself entering the post-war era was the product of one extraordinary man, whose life is chronicled in a later chapter—Sir William McLintock, who bestrode the inter-war years of the firm like the proverbial colossus. What was in his day the personal fiefdom of a great chieftain of the accountancy world, which the Glasgow office in effect declined to join, preferring for the time a quiet but independent life, has had to be turned round through one hundred and eighty degrees to meet contemporary conditions.

In the process, the relationship between the firm's Scottish roots and its south-of-the-border ramifications has also changed, though not in expected ways. For many years Scotland used to export large numbers of accountants to London and elsewhere; even today, more than half the partners in the London office are Scottish CAs. But the flow southwards is not what it was. Conversely, the Glasgow office has recently been at least as active as the rest of the business, expanding through mergers across Scotland to make it what must now be the largest firm in Scotland. If there is rather a startling contrast between the elegantly modern and comfortably carpeted offices of the new McLintock building in the City of London, and the slightly spartan but very human atmosphere of the Victorian terrace houses that comprise the Glasgow office, then that contrast no longer reflects, as it might once have done, the relative dynamism of the respective partnerships.

The centenary year of Thomson McLintock is after all really the centenary of the Scottish parent office, and it is therefore appropriate, though hardly planned, that it should have been marked by such a burst of activity in Scotland. What is more, the story of that century is very much the story of a series of remarkable Scotsmen, in and out of Scotland, who created Thomson McLintock & Co and made it, for good or ill, what it is today; and the first of those Scotsmen was Thomson McLintock himself.

PART I

Chapter One

MR THOMSON McLINTOCK

THOMSON MCLINTOCK founded the firm that bears his name in 1877 in Glasgow, at the age of 26. The precise origins of the McLintock family are not known, but it is thought that they came from Ireland; according to legend, a McLintock came over to Scotland in a cattle boat and settled in the south of Scotland. He was accompanied by a group of other adventurous Irishmen who also settled in the district around Dumfries.

Thomson McLintock's father, William, became a house factor or estate agent and appears to have had a reasonably successful business in Dumfries and district. He married Mary Roberton and lived with his family in Sanquhar, Dumfriesshire. Thomson McLintock was born there in 1851, the younger son in a family of nine children, seven of whom were girls, and was educated at Dumfries Academy. His elder brother died at the age of 22, never having married.

To the modern eye, perhaps the most surprising thing is that, as far as is known, Thomson McLintock did not receive any formal training as an accountant and did not pass any examinations as such. In a certificate of advertisement dated 1879 by the publishers of the *North British Daily Mail*, regarding the sale of house property in which he was acting, he was described simply as 'accountant'. His obituary states that 'He received his training as an accountant in the office of Norrie & Anderson, Glasgow', who were thought to have been in the textile trade, 'and subsequently in that of the late James L Selkirk, CA, Glasgow'.

The term 'accountant' was freely used at that time in Scotland. As H Woolf, in his *Short History of Accountants and Accountancy* (1912) says, 'A great deal of accountant's work was formerly in Scotland performed by solicitors and it is not uncommon to find the legal term "writer" and the designation of "accountant" applied to one and the same person. Scottish merchants were also sometimes spoken of as "accountants" and we also meet with instances of the latter term being used to designate those who were really teachers of book-keeping.'

However, after Thomson had set up practice on his own in Glasgow, he was admitted in 1880 as an associate member of the Institute of Chartered Accountants in England and Wales at the time of its incorporation by Royal Charter. If this also seems surprising, it must be remembered that there were at that time three separate chartered institutes of accountants in Scotland, which were only amalgamated in 1951 to form The Institute of Chartered Accountants of Scotland, and membership of them was at first extremely strictly regulated. One result was that in Glasgow, in about 1890, an influential body of accountants who were not members of the existing chartered bodies put pressure on the restrictive practice of those institutions by proposing to form a chartered society to be known as the 'Scottish Institute'; they formally petitioned the Privy Council.

Naturally, strong objection was taken by the three existing Scottish chartered societies and the petition was refused. However, in 1890 the council of the Institute of Accountants and Actuaries in Glasgow took the view 'that the time had come for opening the door of admission to well qualified men, the course of whose preliminary training had not conformed in all respects to what is required of young men joining in the ordinary way'. In arriving at this conclusion the council was to a considerable extent influenced by the recommendation of Robert Finlay QC, that, if the 'Scottish Institute's application were rejected, steps should be taken with a view to admission into the chartered bodies of such of the petitioners for the

Mr Thomson McLintock in his library at 'Glendyne'

'Glendyne', the home of Mr Thomson McLintock

TELEPHONE No 803.

THOMSON McLINTOCK.
CHARTERED ACCOUNTANT.

88 St Vincent Street.

Glasgow. 24th Mch 1898

John Henderson Esq.
Solicitor
Dumfries

My Dear Sir,

I received your favour of 21st curt,

I have been for many years Auditor of the Sanquhar District Savings Bank, but its operations are very limited as compared with the Dumfries Savings Bank. The work of Audit will however proceed upon similar lines and be directed to a thorough check of the Treasurer's Intromissions dealing with the Income received from Monies lodged by the Depositors and the Revenue from the Investments, and on the other hand the Withdrawals by Depositors and all the other Disbursements in connection with the Bank's Business. I do not know whether it would be practicable, as in the case of smaller Banks, to call in Depositors Pass Books in order to check these with the Bank Ledgers. If this could be done it would certainly be the most satisfactory plan to adopt in making a thorough examination of the Books, although, of course, the Depositors have an opportunity of verifying from their Pass Books the correctness of the sum at the credit of each in the Ledgers from the printed List of Balances published at the end of each financial year.

If the Directors would rather have the Fee fixed before making the appointment I am willing to undertake the duties at Twenty five guineas per annum.

Yours faithfully,

Thomas McClintock

TWO PAGES OF A SUBMISSION OF SUITABILITY – 1898

Sir William McLintock

charter as might fairly be considered to be bona fide practising accountants'.

A new rule providing for such admission was duly made in 1891. Under this rule an application was submitted by Thomson McLintock for admission, and it was unanimously agreed to recommend him to the quarterly general meeting; at this meeting, held on the same day, he was duly elected. He was thus in the then unique position of holding the diploma of both the English and the Glasgow institutes.

When he set up his own firm fourteen years earlier, in 1877, Thomson McLintock had already married Jeannie Marshall, but she had died leaving one son, the future Sir William McLintock, who was born in 1873 and is always referred to in the private ledger as Willie. Following the death of his first wife, Thomson remarried and Mary Agnes McKinnell became the mother of two more sons, TL McLintock and Charles McLintock, and three daughters, Ina, Jean and Mary. All three of the sons appear as members of the firm; William as a dominant figure in the accountancy world in London, TL McLintock as senior partner in Glasgow for a period of years, and Charles in the London firm, though his career was somewhat disjointed by work in the Ministry of Munitions during the 1914–1918 war and by work in industry. Two of the daughters also had an indirect connection with the firm. Jean married Norman Sinclair of Robert Sinclair & Co, Tobacco Merchants of Newcastle-upon-Tyne, and this firm's accounts and the family's private financial affairs were handled for a period by the McLintock firm. Mary married William Fraser, subsequently the first Lord Strathalmond, who was manager of Pumpherston Oil Company at the time when Thomson McLintock was a director and chairman of that company. This was to prove a very important personal connection later, for Pumpherston Oil Company developed via Scottish Shale Oil into a part of BP.

Throughout the early history of the firm there is a strong family connection. Not only do the sons feature, but also

William McLintock senior was associated for many years. The first business associate was an unidentified R McLintock, thought to have been an uncle or cousin. His name appears only during the first seven years 1877–1883. Another relation by marriage was William Gilmour, who features in the accounts of the business from 1878. Thomson McLintock's sister Annie (born 1886, died 1933) married into the Gilmour family and in the private ledger the name of Gilmour appears repeatedly. Though he was one of Thomson McLintock's earliest business associates, William Gilmour apparently also never qualified as an accountant, but was referred to as such.

The private ledger gives infinite details of Thomson McLintock's personal expenditure during these years. Here are to be found the clues to the everyday life of a Victorian businessman rising to an eminent position. Coal bills are paid, the shrubbery laid out, the family increases in number and in expense. Mrs McLintock only receives small sums of money, for Thomson McLintock himself deals with all the housekeeping items. He buys hats and ulsters, and pays subscriptions. Soirées are attended, innumerable lantern slides are hired. One son, William, has athletic proclivities, so there is an item 'to Willie's tennis coaching'; another son is musical, so we find 'Tom's violin lessons', and 'Tom's singing lessons'. These activities on the part of the sons point to characteristics of the father, for Thomson McLintock was reputed to have been to the end of his days a great walker, to have had musical interests and, in later life, to have taken up that essential pastime of chartered accountants, golf. In earlier years he purchased bowls and took a half share in a tricycle. Though railway fares do appear there is little mention of any other form of transport, apart from a very occasional reference to the hiring of a carriage.

To a modern reader, it is quite remarkable that a businessman of Thomson McLintock's calibre should have had the industry and precision to record such minutiae. Presumably, this was a Victorian habit. The record is exact and the entries in the private journal balance whenever and wherever they have been checked.

The first offices were at 87 St Vincent Street, Glasgow, and this number 87 was later changed by the Post Office to 88. The main sources of income were accounting and bankruptcy fees. The general impression is that Thomson McLintock formed his primary reputation as an accountant in Glasgow as the result of his handling of catastrophes relating to the City of Glasgow Bank crash in 1878. It must be recollected that he was a man of undisputed probity with strong principles (also strongly religious—for many years he belonged to a sect called the Church of Christ). These qualities, added to ability as an accountant and a toughness required for such work, would attract attention at such a time. This type of work set the pattern upon which the firm's London reputation was later to be substantially based. In 1908 he was appointed to an official committee to look into the bankruptcy laws of Scotland.

A very revealing story is recorded by KG Harvey. Apparently, Thomson McLintock told the young Harvey that he should never be too theoretical, always be practical, and he illustrated this by saying that in one of the first sequestrations he handled, that of a grocer's business, the main asset was stock. Had this been sold on the usual bankruptcy lines there would have been very little for the creditors. Thomson McLintock therefore decided that he would keep the shop open and sell the stock at retail prices. He himself rolled up his sleeves, went behind the counter and sold the groceries with the result that the creditors received a far better dividend than they ever expected. Thereafter all these creditors insisted on having Thomson McLintock as the trustee in any bankruptcy in which they were involved.

In 1901 the office transferred to 149 West George Street, from 88 St Vincent Street. It would seem, although no document exists to prove it, that in 1901 a copartnery agreement was entered into. The advent of qualified sons no doubt necessitated a fresh start. It is apparent that, whether there was a formal agreement, regular divisions of net profits and the provision by the recipients of some capital sum was established in 1901. The firm's accounts at the beginning of this period show that the net profits were divided:

Thomson McLintock	3/6
William McLintock	1/6
William Gilmour	1/6
TL McLintock	1/6

The capital account remained the same from 1901 to 1911:

Thomson McLintock	£600
William McLintock	£200
William Gilmour	£200
TL McLintock	£200

It would appear that Thomson McLintock provided the two sums of £200 for his sons.

In 1911 a formal contract of copartnery was signed and this may well have been the first formal agreement entered into: it was for a period of five years from 1 January 1911 to 31 December 1915, and its details were:

	Capital	*Division of profits*	*Salaries*
Thomson McLintock	£400	2/5	£600
William McLintock	£400	2/5	£500
TL McLintock	£200	1/5	£500
William Gilmour	£200	5% of profits over £2,000	£400

There was an additional clause binding the firm to pay £150 per annum for life to William McLintock senior, Thomson's father, whether he was an employee or not.

Charles McLintock, the youngest son of Thomson McLintock, qualified as a chartered accountant in December 1912, having served his apprenticeship with the Glasgow firm. In 1914 he went to London and remained in England throughout the rest of his career. He appears never to have been a partner in the Glasgow firm, at least to the extent of receiving a proportion of the profits and providing capital. What happened was that in 1914 William and Charles McLintock went to London together as the result of a winding-up order appointing Thomson McLintock liquidator of the Northern Equitable Insurance Company Limited. Most of the staff of the Northern Equitable were dismissed on liquidation, but some were retained by McLintocks. Among them was Andrew Black, who in 1959 compiled his recollections of the firm.

He remembered Thomson McLintock sitting at the end of the long board-room table at 149 West George Street, looking very impressive with white hair, large white moustache, bolt upright—'an upright man in every sense of the word. To see him conduct a meeting of shareholders or the like was a sight to be remembered; he dominated the meeting and proceedings were conducted with a dignity enough to strike awe into anyone who might have come with the idea of being difficult. He was always in complete control, never ruffled and always courtesy itself. Towards the staff, Thomson McLintock displayed another side of his character. He was very approachable and easy to talk with; it was quite usual for him to walk into the general office and stop to chat with different members of staff. He was also known on occasions to take out his sovereign case (which all gentlemen carried at the end of their watch chains in those days) and quietly present a golden sovereign to some member of the staff whose work had pleased him.

'Mr McLintock was always very reluctant to take any legal action against debtors or against shareholders owing calls on their shares. Any kind of compromise or arrangement for payment by instalments would find favour with him rather than the issue of a writ. "I am here to liquidate not to litigate" was his favourite expression and, looking back with more experience, one cannot help feeling he was right, although it did not always appear so at the time.

'In those days it was quite common for accountants in Scotland to combine accountancy with other activities – many were stockbrokers. Thomson McLintock & Co were house factors and insurance agents and, incredible though it may seem, Thomson McLintock's father, who must have been over 80, insisted on coming to the office "to assist his son" with the work in the house factoring department and would let no one prevent him. The writer sat next to him at the same high desk in the general office and so can claim to have worked with four generations of McLintocks.'

TC Guthrie, who joined the Glasgow firm about 1913 and transferred to London in 1919, ultimately becoming senior partner in the Manchester firm in 1933, remembered this about the Glasgow office:

'In 1913, there was among the clerical staff an odd character, McKim, whose main job was to rule all the accounts and statements typed on the Elliott-Fisher machine, in red ink lines for £ s d – a job requiring great art and patience. McKim must, in his time, have ruled thousands of miles in red ink! He was "in a class by himself". He lived in the YMCA but knew when the pubs opened and then kept well away from TMcL.' McKim was still with the firm and hand-ruling accounts in 1935.

Andrew Black added to the picture of the office: 'At the time all accounts and reports were typed on large paper on the flat Elliott-Fisher machine, and bound with silk ribbon in legal fashion; all rulings were done by hand.

'The copying press was still in use in the Glasgow office in 1914 and someone had the messy job of copying all letters into letter books with the use of damp cloths. Within the following year or so Kenrick and Jefferson's letter sets were introduced but there had to be two copies of each letter for, while Mr McLintock was willing to give way to Mr William's new-fangled notions, he was not willing to give up his letter books and one copy of each letter had to be bound up in letter book style with an index, a practice which continued for many years. Mr McLintock found the letter books useful for keeping in touch with what was going on in the office and as an indication of the volume of work in fixing fees for certain jobs.'

TC Guthrie recollected that in the years after about 1910:

'Thomson McLintock left a great deal of the work to his two elder sons and, although regularly at the office, took a minor part in the firm's work. He was completely frank and open about this and would honestly tell a client, whom he met by chance in the street and who made inquiry about his work or affairs, that "my son, William, is dealing with your affairs now and there is no point in my trying to answer you. Go and see William".'

Guthrie also provided the best summing up of this remarkable man:

'Thomson McLintock was greatly loved and respected by his staff in the latter years of his working life. He had great natural dignity, kindliness and humanity and perfect sincerity. He had no humbug and no side. In fact, one of his tales was to the effect that when some rather sidy client or friend inquired where Thomson McLintock's daughters had finished their education, expecting him to say Paris or Switzerland, the reply was "In the kitchen beside their mother". Thomson McLintock was a teetotaller and non-smoker, except for an odd cigar. In short, he might be described as the best type of puritan, brought up in Victorian days, a type of man quite extinct.'

Chapter Two

PARTING OF THE WAYS

As long as Thomson McLintock was alive he remained the authoritative figure in the firm, even though he delegated most of the work to his sons in his later years. However, his death in January 1920 heralded a change, with increasing tension between the Glasgow and London offices during the 1920s and 1930s leading to an eventual split in 1934. In part, this conflict can be explained by the very different characters of the two half-brothers, William McLintock and TL McLintock, and in part by the increasing importance of London as a business centre. Although for many years the fiction was maintained that Glasgow was head office, nevertheless the accounts record the meteoric rise of the London business with nothing comparable happening in Glasgow. This chapter therefore chronicles the story of the separation and divorce of the two offices; the next chapter will consider in detail Sir William's achievements in London.

Thomson McLintock's death led to a new contract of copartnery being established in March 1921. Four new partners were appointed. The capital account, division of profits and salaries paid were:

	Capital		*Division*	
	1921–23	*From 1923*	*of profits*	*Salaries*
W McLintock	£8,600	£17,200	43%	£3,000
TL McLintock	3,700	7,400	18½%	1,000
J Duncan	3,700	7,400	18½%	800
JC Burleigh	800	1,600	4%	600

W Anderson	600	1,200	3%	500
HE Borland	600	1,200	3%	500
J Morison	600	1,200	3%	500

Note: The balance of 7% was held as 'reserved' for discretionary division as the three senior partners thought appropriate.

William McLintock therefore remained as a senior partner, despite being mainly in London, but his half-brother TL McLintock, was, together with John Duncan, in charge of the Glasgow office, which in 1918 had been transferred to 216 West George Street. William McLintock remained a partner in Glasgow throughout, though after 1928 he was not receiving any remuneration from the Scottish firm. In fact, this continued to be the situation up to the time of his death in 1947.

Prior to the 1914–1918 war the firm's business in London meant much travelling to and fro, mainly on the part of William McLintock. The pace accelerated after the Budget of 1909, and in 1914 an office was opened permanently in London with Charles McLintock in charge. William McLintock was from the start much involved in the London business and supervised his youngest brother's work in the first London office; at the same time, however, he was still concerned with the Glasgow work. Nevertheless, by 1917 the pressure of work and the loss of time involved in the constant travelling necessitated a change. William McLintock went south and took full-time control of the London office. During the latter part of the war years and even into the early 1920s, there was still much movement between the two offices. It became a common statement that 'so and so' had his season ticket to London. John Morison first appears in 1919 as one of the frequent travellers and he continued to make the journey until he settled in London in 1926.

It should be recorded that prior to the 1914–1918 war, when the pace of life was slower and communications were more leisurely, the pattern of business was much more de-centralized than it is today. After the war, however, there was a marked move towards London. Businesses and individuals, who would once have accepted as natural an accountant or other adviser in a provincial city, joined in a fashionable surge to London. Firms such as Thomson McLintock & Co, Glasgow, who were well established, were not over-much affected; nevertheless, the fact that McLintocks had a London office established at that period was of great value and the cream of the work during the 1920s and early 1930s went there. Thomson McLintock & Co were one of the first Scottish accounting firms to open an office in London.

In the early days, the London office did obtain work and contacts through the Glasgow office; but as Sir William became established, it began to stand on its own feet and attained great success. In 1919 gross fees in Glasgow were £28,000 and in London £13,000. By 1927 these figures were £45,000 and £102,000 respectively, and by 1933 £37,000 and £159,000.

This change in the centre of gravity naturally affected the attitude both of the 'old firm' in Glasgow and of the 'new firm' in London and there are on record numerous exchanges between the two offices which became increasingly divergent in view until, in March 1934, the problem was solved by separation. As well as actual conflict, there is evidence in the early 1920s of simple confusion. A letter from William McLintock to TL McLintock dated 14 November 1921 ('written in train') accompanying London office accounts as at 31 August 1921 and returning Glasgow office draft accounts states: 'I got a shock when trying to reconcile the G/O and L/O accounts by discovering that a sum at my debit at 31 August 1920, of almost £1,700 had not been put through your books' (that is, the Glasgow books). 'I made the J/E in London on 1 September 1920, and evidently forgot to advise you.' The same letter goes on to say: 'The London results are surprisingly good for the short time the business has been in existence and it will be difficult to maintain same when the big taxation fees cease.' Another partner is required in London, but William McLintock makes it clear that he wishes to keep the door open for one of his own young men.

Later in the same month, November 1921, William McLintock writes to TL McLintock and mentions the wish for a copy of the Glasgow accounts but does not want to put TL to the trouble of making copies of the final accounts 'with your own hand'. Could he have a copy if such is being typed? TL McLintock makes factual and businesslike replies but it is already apparent that William McLintock is calling the tune. Occasionally, detailed criticism and some measure of praise are meted out, as in 1922: 'Burleigh sent me your profit and loss account which is very satisfactory and I hope you can maintain it, although with taxation and coal (not coal industry) such a large item with a low expense ratio I doubt it.' In the same letter there is criticism of TL's bonus to staff which is 'much too low, a little less than 1% of the total fees. Between holiday and special we give four times as much in London.'

By the early 1930s other figures enter the lists; JC Burleigh, John Duncan and John Morison correspond on the knotty question of the division of profits. 'It is a somewhat troubled story. The original suggestion was a percentage of the *total* profits on the following scale. In London we amended this by converting TL and W McLintock on to a percentage of the London profits . . . JD was given the option of settling on a basis of 6% of Glasgow profits or ¼% of the whole . . .'

Various efforts were made to come to terms but the trend is clear. More serious misunderstandings involving allocation of time between the two offices, the use of principal's time, fees charged and other matters became increasingly important. A memorandum dated 9 December 1931 from London to Glasgow is very firm '. . . and regret to note you have been labouring under the misapprehension that all the work in the above matter has been done from the Glasgow office . . . The facts are as stated in my previous memo, that all the "really troublesome work" is in fact done at this end, and whatever may be *our* ideas on the matter there is no doubt that *our clients* regard the matter as being in the personal charge of Sir William at this end.'

In January 1931, London, in the person of JC Burleigh, puts forward a fresh argument that 'I do not think that the services rendered should be solely based on time spent by reason of the fact that not only was the value of the introduction worth something, but Sir William's friendship with the directors of the controlling company, and to a lesser extent, my knowledge of the undertaking and its connections, were of considerable value throughout the negotiations'. On this occasion London proposed a separate fee (of 750gns). 'This should be rendered quite separately of any fee for work done in Glasgow office, as all the negotiations of importance and the heavy end of the work were done here.' Lip service is, however, done to the fact that the client 'came to London with – in a sense – a note of introduction from Glasgow'. The letter ends, 'If you prefer, we shall render our account direct leaving you to render the Glasgow fee separately.'

In February of the next year, 1932, Sir William wrote a long and detailed letter to John Duncan which is marked 'Personal':

'I received your letter of 28 ultimo, enclosing the time sheet in connection with the above matter.

'The method in which you have dealt with this time raises an important question from our point of view in London. In the first place, the inter-office rates for principals are, in my opinion, too high, as they represent probably as high or possibly higher rates than would be charged by the Glasgow office to their clients in the ordinary way.

'This work was entrusted to me in London, and I received a pretty clear indication that it was not simply to be turned over to our Glasgow office, and as far as possible that request was duly acted upon. If for work arising as this did, and of the same character, such high rates are to be charged, it would, from the mere financial standpoint, pay us to send our own staff from here and bear out of our fee any travelling and living expenses incurred. The same attitude was adopted in regard to the X matter where there was, in my opinion, an undue expenditure of principals' time, and while I am anxious —and all the other partners here are of the same mind—to send business to the Glasgow office, we cannot continue to do so if the work secured in London and performed in Glasgow is to be remunerated at the inter-office rates you have recently adopted.

'This whole question raises the issue that in the Glasgow office you have not got a sufficient number of fully qualified capable senior men to do work which apparently must devolve on partners. I have raised this question before, but in doing work for London I think it is only reasonable to recognize that you do not balance your staff as we do here, and therefore any charge included in inter-office rates must have regard to that fact. I do not know if you accept the principle that in strict inter-office work the rates should not be the same as if you were working direct for a client. They should be of such an amount that a profit is left on the time to be charged to clients by the office where the work originated.

'Ever yours, Willie.

'PS. Don't for one minute think I am reflecting on the excellent work by Dowling.'

Perusal of the firm's accounts in Glasgow shows that the final joint accounts were produced for the year ending 31 March 1927. Thereafter the two firms acted as independent units and, on 1 April 1934, a complete separation of the two firms was established. In that year a contract of copartnery was executed by the Glasgow firm, the partners being Sir William McLintock, TL McLintock and J Duncan (the three being the senior partners), William Anderson, JT Dowling, HE Borland, TC Currie and JH Haddow. It was provided in this contract that the business in Scotland was to be carried on entirely separately from the business outside Scotland. However, nothing was to prevent the London firm from carrying on business in Scotland (Clause 6). Sir William retained certain clients in Scotland to the end of his life and these clients insisted on his imprimatur on their company audits. A famous and annual event for Sir William was an audit in the north of Scotland with lunch (essentially including apple dumpling) and golf at the Cruden Bay Hotel.

It is to the career of this powerful, high-living man that we must now turn.

Chapter Three

SIR WILLIAM McLINTOCK

1914–1921

WILLIAM MCLINTOCK was, as we have seen, the eldest son of Thomson McLintock and the only child of his first marriage. He was born on 26 September 1873, but his mother died during his infancy and his father remarried fairly quickly. He was brought up in Sanquhar with his younger half-brothers and sisters and attended Dumfries Academy; later, when the family moved to Glasgow, he went to Glasgow High School.

The home atmosphere of the McLintock family appears to have been happy, though to modern eyes somewhat puritanical. In his youth, William had ample opportunity to develop his interest in sport and music. He was devoted to his stepmother and visited her regularly towards the end of her life. Obviously, from all records and recollection, William McLintock was a most charming and attractive man. Though not himself brilliant intellectually (apparently he had to sit the final examination more than once before qualifying, and certainly he was not one of the large number of members of the firm who obtained distinction or prizes) he developed a keen business sense, was very social, knew how to make friends with the right people and had an exceptional gift for attracting able people to work for him. He was a member of the Orpheus Club in Glasgow and enjoyed acting and singing, particularly in Gilbert and Sullivan operas. There is a report that his father had cause to take William to task over his work, and to tell him that he must make up his mind whether to make a career as a singer or as an accountant. Apparently singing was relegated to the status of hobby thereafter, for accountant he became, qualifying in 1896 as a member of the Institute of Accountants and Actuaries in Glasgow after serving his apprenticeship with Thomson McLintock. Music remained a great interest and relaxation in William McLintock's life. For instance, during the period 1917 to 1921, when he had furnished a flat in London where he stayed during the week, he always hired a piano.

When William McLintock entered the Glasgow firm in 1896, the business was thriving. Thomson McLintock was a much respected figure and the firm's name stood in high repute. William was assumed as a partner in 1901. It is interesting to speculate how this lively and ambitious man managed as time went on to curb his energies in such a way as to comply with the now elderly Thomson McLintock. One can only assume that early discipline and puritanical training for a long time made him feel that it was his duty to remain in Glasgow. Interestingly, when the move in the direction of London came, it seems to have been the cause of tension between William and his father. It does not seem at all unlikely that Thomson McLintock knew that William was the son who could most help him in his business and that he therefore deliberately kept him in Glasgow and gradually passed over important clients to him. Meanwhile, William became thoroughly versed in the business, matured and made contacts. He may have had the vision to see the beginning of the trend for business to congregate in London and to know that Thomson McLintock & Co would soon have to go there too.

The event which led to the opening of a London office was the appointment of Thomson McLintock as liquidator of the Northern Equitable Insurance Company in January 1914. The Northern Equitable Insurance Company was registered in Scotland but moved its head office from Glasgow to London towards the end of 1912. It was one of several comparatively small companies which had been floated to take advantage of the widened scope for insurance created by the Workmen's Compensation Act, 1906. Most of these companies sooner or

Mr Thomson Liddell McLintock

1

Private Journal. 1877

75	Ferguson McEwan & Co. Dr.	3	.			
	Writing up books & preparing Balance					
1 PL	To Accountant Com a/c Cr				3	.
365	Fallas & Co. Dfs Dr.	12	12	.		
	Opening New Set of books by D.E. & Writing up books.					
PL/1	To Acct Com a/c Cr				12	12
365	James Frew Dr.	5	5	.		
	Opening New Set of books & preparing State of Affairs					
PL/1	To Acct Com a/c Cr				5	5
382	D Wilson & Co. Dr.	2	2			
	Opening New Set of books & framing Deed of Agreement					
PL/1	To Accountant Com a/c Cr				2	2
					22	19

2

773	Macleod Adam & Co Dr	5 5 .	
	Writing up books & preparing State of your affairs		
/1	To Accountant Com a/c Cr		5 5
87	John Wright Esq Dr	4 4 .	
	Preparing Balance Sheet as at 31/1/77.		
/1	To Account. Com a/c Cr		4 4 .
9	N Union Life Dr	2 . 8.	
	For Com on Prem till 20/3/77.		
/7	To Com a/c (NU) Cr		2 . 8
2	D Wilson & Co Dr	2 2 .	
	Framing Deed of Agreement		
/1	To Com a/c - Acct. Cr		2 2
			36 10 8

THE OPENING ENTRIES – 1877

Mr John Duncan

later went the same way as the Northern Equitable. No doubt this particular firm had rather grand ideas, for it established itself in a new building called Equitable House in King William Street. However, it had not been long in occupation before the Court of Session, Edinburgh, on 14 January 1914, made a winding-up order, appointing Thomson McLintock as liquidator.

Following the winding-up order, as we have seen, Thomson McLintock's two sons, William and Charles, went south to take charge of the liquidation. The work of liquidation continued until the end of 1916. It was necessary to maintain a small office and staff in London to collect debts and settle claims in connection with the substantial part of the Northern Equitable business in the south. The office in Equitable House was too large and expensive for the purpose and little time was lost in disclaiming the lease and finding a smaller office. Early in March 1914 an office was taken in the name of Thomson McLintock & Co at 158 Fenchurch Street. This was a small office on the third floor of a then modern building and contained four rather small rooms. The rent amounted to £465 per annum which, in accordance with City practice at that time, included rates, heating and cleaning. It is possible that the office was taken over from Gulbenkian Ltd, which may have been the start of the firm's long association with CS Gulbenkian, the oil millionaire who became known as 'Mr Five Per Cent'; this association later led to the opening of the Lisbon office.

The firm showed no lack of confidence in opening its first London office, for it at once ordered a large, made-to-order cash book of 250 folios with Scottish rulings, which seems to indicate that it had every intention of remaining in London after the Northern Equitable was wound up.

The staff were mainly Northern Equitable employees whose salaries were charged to the liquidation together with about three-quarters of the office rent. The salary bill was £35 to £40 per month to start with and fell to £12. 10. 0d by September 1916, after which no further charge to the

Northern Equitable for salaries appears to have been made. While, upon the Northern Equitable going into liquidation, most of the staff had to be dismissed, some of the accounts and claims staff retained for the liquidation work eventually transferred to the firm's staff and remained for many years. The most notable names among this group were Andrew Black himself, DL Smith and RH Still. DL Smith had worked in the motor claims department of Northern Equitable: 'He soon learned to turn his hand to all sorts of work once he joined Thomson McLintock & Co.' After war service, he returned to the firm and remained until 1943. Originally, he was particularly involved with trade association work, particularly for the lead and subsequently the milling industries.

RH Still acted as cashier and book-keeper and did most of the administrative work in the office. He also assisted with, and eventually was wholly engaged on, professional work until, for health reasons, he left the firm in 1925 to take a job in the country. His health restored, he took up the study of cost accounting and later held important positions in industrial concerns, finally becoming a director of Bakelite Limited.

Andrew Black in effect set up the London office and, though not himself a chartered accountant, remained a pillar of the firm until he left in 1947 to take an appointment with the British Transport Commission.

The three years until the Northern Equitable liquidation work in London was completed towards the end of 1916, can be regarded as the first phase in the early history of the London office. The outbreak of war in August 1914 no doubt hampered the development of the firm's professional practice in London and during the first three years the work was largely, but not wholly, concerned with the Northern Equitable liquidation. Soon after the outbreak of war, probably early 1915, Charles McLintock joined the staff of the Ministry of Munitions under Mark Webster Jenkinson, FCA. They were engaged on costing work in connection with the Government's war-time shell-filling factories; costing at that time was only just coming into its own as a branch of accountancy.

Charles McLintock was later awarded an OBE for his services.

The work of second importance to the Northern Equitable liquidation was probably that arising under the Trading with the Enemy Act, 1914, and subsequent amendments. The Board of Trade appointed William McLintock personally to investigate, supervise and, sometimes, wind-up German-owned businesses. The most important of these appointments was that in connection with H Huber and Company, a firm of paper merchants of which H Huber was the sole proprietor. He was forced to sell his business, which he did to two of his British employees, Messrs Wardill and Gilbert, and the company's name changed accordingly. McLintocks became auditors of the new firm, dealt with the tax affairs of the new partners and, for many years after, acted for Henry Huber and his family in connection with their tax and financial affairs. An interesting sequel to this story is recalled by TC Guthrie: 'After all these years there is probably no harm in recording an uncomfortable incident which befell TCG in the office of Wardill & Gilbert. The firm was in serious trouble with the Inland Revenue authorities as they had omitted to enter large receipts in their books from the sale of paper licences during the 1914–1918 war. There was the threat of a criminal prosecution hanging over the partners but, in the end, Thomson McLintock & Co settled the matter on the basis of tax lost, plus a heavy penalty. TCG was handling the job and at a meeting with the partners, Wardill, who was a nervous wreck and in a distracted state of mind, produced suddenly, from a drawer in his desk, a loaded revolver and threatened to blow his brains out. It was with the greatest difficulty and much "wind-up" that Gilbert and TCG managed to calm Wardill down a bit and get him to hand over the revolver, which Gilbert promptly locked up.'

Following the completion of the Northern Equitable liquidation and towards the end of 1916, William McLintock jointly with Harry Peat of Peat Marwick Mitchell & Co was engaged to advise on a merger of explosives companies headed by Nobel's Explosives Limited (referred to as NEM). The NEM work was almost certainly due to William McLintock's friendship with Harry (later Lord) McGowan, a Glasgow neighbour and chairman of the company. From this merger stemmed a good deal of tax work amongst the NEM constituent companies and many useful contacts, which William McLintock was very able to exploit.

Indeed, for a proper understanding of the significance of Sir William's and the firm's activity in those years, it is necessary for the modern reader to realize that accountants then performed much the same role as merchant banks do today—that is, they advised on and arranged mergers and 'acted for' commercial companies in special situations. Accountancy firms, particularly in England rather than in Scotland, have now to a considerable degree lost this role to the merchant banks. But this was largely a development of the post-second world war period. In the twenties Sir William virtually relied on this type of business to sustain the firm in London, and it was only at the close of the twenties that a special audit manager was appointed, with the realization that 'special jobs' were too unpredictable and that the London firm needed to develop the 'bread and butter' of audit work.

NEM could therefore be regarded as the forerunner of the big business in company mergers which was such a feature of McLintocks' activities in the period following the first world war. The work occupied about two years and, during this period, the affairs of the merging companies were investigated in considerable detail. The modern technique of the takeover bid had not then been developed. Eventually, in 1918, Explosives Trades Limited was formed as a holding company to acquire the shares of the merging companies. During the 1920s, the name was changed to Nobel Industries Limited; later a further merger took place between Nobel Industries Limited and Brunner Mond & Company Limited and, in 1926, the name became Imperial Chemical Industries Limited. Thomson McLintock & Co is still joint auditor (with Price Waterhouse) of ICI.

The first secretary of Explosives Trades Limited was Dr Josiah Stamp. He came from the Inland Revenue, was a close friend of William McLintock and it is likely that William McLintock introduced him to McGowan. Soon after the merger Stamp conceived the idea of preparing consolidated accounts. TMcL were instructed to prepare 'merger balance sheets' for each of the companies at the date of merging, ie balance sheets based on the merger valuations, and, in due course, a consolidated balance sheet was produced by Explosives Trades Limited. Consolidated accounts are now common form, but in 1919/20 it was pioneering work. It is probable that Explosives Trades Limited or Nobel Industries Limited were the first to publish consolidated accounts, some thirty years before 'group accounts' became compulsory under the 1948 Companies Act.

Early in 1918, the firm moved to larger offices at Bond Court House, Walbrook, where it remained until March 1923, when new offices at 71 Queen Street were acquired. The Bond Court office was palatial compared to 158 Fenchurch Street. There was a board-room, a large room for William McLintock with an adjacent room for secretaries, a room for typists and a general office with seating for perhaps a dozen. This office had high sloping desks and tall stools. Once again one suspects an element of foresight. The war, though not yet over, was drawing to an end and with the cessation of hostilities there was every possibility that business would expand. Though William McLintock was thought to have been over-optimistic in taking on such a large office, by May 1919 it was proving too small and the firm took over the semi-basement in the same building. The rent for these combined offices was £800/£840 (the variable figure being accounted for by the rates and services). Obviously the offices were furnished and fitted in considerable style, for Maple & Company, who did most of the work and supplied the greater part of the furniture, submitted an account in excess of £1,000, a large sum of money for 1918.

Another sign of rising prosperity—and of the grand style

that became his personal characteristic—was that William seems to have acquired his first motor car in the early months of 1919. It was a second-hand Siddeley-Deasy which he bought from Rotax Motor Accessories Co for £645 and he had a very smart chauffeuse, Miss Perritt, to drive it. He sold it in September 1920 for £675 and bought a new Armstrong-Siddeley for £1,120—again a large sum in those days.

After the move to Bond Court House the practice built up rapidly and the staff increased, particularly after the end of the war. At this time several figures who later rose to eminence in the firm, enter the scene. Gerald Bradley, later to become senior partner in London in 1967–68, became the firm's first indentured apprentice in late 1917. JC Burleigh was demobilized from the army in May 1919 and came straight into the firm. He became a partner in 1920 and senior partner from 1947 to 1954. Another important entrant was FJ Cooksey, who joined the firm from the Inland Revenue early in 1920. It has been said that William McLintock was very aware of the increasing importance of taxation work at this time and that with his usual astuteness 'he brought or even some say bought' Cooksey as a specialist to run this department. Cooksey was articled to William McLintock but never in fact qualified as a chartered accountant. He remained with the firm for many years and always held a rather special position, being very well paid. He retired in 1944.

An interesting light is thrown on the wider value of this tax expertise by TC Guthrie. He considered that 'the specialization in taxation was probably the most important factor in the great expansion of the firm for the fifty years following the establishment of the London office in 1914. High taxation from 1914 onwards meant that large sums of money were involved and expert knowledge and advice could ensure large savings. William McLintock was one of the first practising accountants in the country to realise this. Probably his first big tax job was to negotiate, about 1914, with the Inland Revenue on behalf of the Lanarkshire coal owners, uniform rates of depreciation on colliery wagons. This was a most successful piece of work and was the beginning of the vast connection with the colliery owners and their associations, not only in Scotland, but in most of the colliery districts in England, culminating in the firm holding the appointment of accountants to the Mining Association of Great Britain and having the largest practice in the colliery industry in the United Kingdom.'

Other figures who came to the London office in the early 1920s were TC Guthrie himself and Duncan McKellar. Both Guthrie and McKellar were transferred from the Glasgow office, together with several other senior staff. Thomas Lister, later senior partner in London, joined the staff in 1921. Charles McLintock left the firm in 1918 and spent many years in industry, becoming a managing director of British Ropes. At Sir William's request, in order to fill the need in London for another senior partner, he returned to the firm in 1934 and remained till his death in January 1947.

John Morison (later Sir John and another eventual senior partner in London) was a frequent visitor to the London office from Glasgow, sometimes for long spells; but he did not make London his headquarters until 1926. During this period the junior staff also increased. Amongst them were Leslie Bell and John Kissane, both of whom subsequently became London partners. At the same time a number of long serving members of the secretarial staff arrived and the first commissionaire, Sergeant Durman, who remained until after the second world war, was engaged.

A considerable amount of additional work came to the London office following the armistice in November 1918. The secretaryships of the various lead associations came to the firm at this time. JC Burleigh carried on the work of the lead department for many years and it was on account of the International White Lead Convention that an office was opened in Paris for a while. This venture was then not very successful and there was never a resident partner. Indeed, the office gossip of the day had it that the Paris office existed to obtain tickets for important clients of the firm to visit the Folies Bergères.

Some of the work that developed in this period was in the Manchester district and, to a large extent, arose out of the British Dyestuffs merger which in turn was a Nobel Industries introduction. TC Guthrie was in charge of it and early in 1919 Harold Bland was engaged as a resident assistant in Manchester. This led to the opening of the Manchester office in 1920; R Paterson became resident partner in 1930 followed by TC Guthrie in 1933 when Paterson left the firm.

From 1919 onwards, the firm also started to handle quite large sums of money for investment on behalf of clients. Underwriting was another activity including an 8% Note Issue in 1920 by Explosives Trades Limited.

JC Burleigh was busy on the affairs of Amalgamated Industrials Limited as well as with the work of the lead department. FJ Cooksey was building up the tax department which had grown at a phenomenal rate and also handled the coal work, which, in the disturbed post-war years, included the calculation of miners' wages.

Duncan McKellar appears on the scene early in 1921 handling liquidation matters. There was a shipbuilding merger which brought a lot of activity in 1921 and involved investigation work in Newcastle, Glasgow and the north of Ireland. Although a great deal of work was put into this job, the merger never in fact took place—perhaps because of the slump which followed the period of prosperity after the war.

By 1921, therefore, the London office had grown to a substantial size, and the scene was set for William McLintock's emergence as one of the three great names of the accountancy profession in the 1920s.

1922–1939

The story of the London office during the 1920s and 1930s is closely bound up with the personal success of William

McLintock. The firm thrived and became one of the most influential in the country.

When Thomson McLintock died in 1920, William was already forty-seven years of age, but the moment was auspicious. Apart from the great upsurge in accountancy work immediately after the 1914–1918 war, the trend for firms to congregate in London accelerated, while taxation and audit work developed enormously; but perhaps there was also an element of pure luck. There was room for a new figure to appear; Lord Plender of Deloitte Plender Griffiths, a famous accountant in his day, was, at the time, much occupied with Treasury and government work: the firm of Price Waterhouse lost its senior partner, Sir Gilbert Garnsey, who died suddenly in his early forties. The field was clear for William McLintock and he was never one to lose an opportunity. In particular, he became a close friend of Lord Plender who had a high opinion of his ability and passed work to him.

Much of the work handled by the London office stemmed directly from William McLintock's advisory activities. For example, he was appointed to overhaul the finances of the Royal Household shortly after the end of the first world war, and after a meticulous examination recommended various useful reforms. This work earned him his knighthood in 1922. He acted as financial advisor to the government in the complex negotiations relating to the numerous road and rail transport facilities in London which led to the creation of the London Passenger Transport Board in 1933; he gave evidence for days on end before a House of Commons select committee and only Stafford Cripps, later to be a Labour Chancellor of the Exchequer, got the better of him. Most important of all was his work in 1928 with Sir Otto Niemeyer as adviser to the Imperial Wireless and Cable Conference, from which merged the huge Cable and Wireless organization.

As his personal prestige rose he was asked to undertake an increasing number of official engagements, such as membership of the Committee on the National Debt in 1924 and the

Royal Commission on Income Tax, 1924 to 1927. In those years few industrial questions were not examined by him as a member of some official body; unemployment insurance, company law amendment, public utility development, cotton, electrification of the railways, broadcasting. He was also a member of the Board of Referees, of the Industrial Arbitration Court, of the Economic Advisory Council, and of the Racecourse Betting Control Board. These special positions were the 'jam' and from them stemmed the 'bread and butter' work of the continuing audits.

Meanwhile other important fields developed and thrived. Taxation, especially after the Royal Commission on Income Tax, brought in a great deal of work and, until 1924, there was a considerable volume of work relating to the Excess Profits Duty imposed during the war. Cooksey was always in the front rank where tax was concerned, and had various innovations to his name. For example, he worked out a skilful scheme during the early 1930s whereby the finances of a group of Roman Catholic convents were organized into charitable trusts. Such trusts have become popular since the second world war but were pioneered in the early 1930s.

Another important field of work in the 1920s was the milling industry. Here again there was an inheritance from the war-time control of the industry during 1914 to 1918. By the mid-1920s the milling industry was fraught with cut-throat competition and in a generally unhealthy state. The great combines, Ranks and Spillers, were asked by their colleagues to take action to remedy the situation. Thomson McLintock & Co were called in and devised a scheme of quotas under the aegis of the Millers Mutual Association. This scheme was very successful and, until the outbreak of the second world war, when once again complete government control was imposed, the industry was organized on this basis. Sir William and Archibald (later Sir Archibald) Forbes took a leading part in these negotiations; subsequently Forbes left the firm to join Spillers, and became its chairman in 1965, as well as becoming a distinguished banker as chairman of the Midland Bank. One may speculate that there was not room in the firm for two men of such clear leadership ability.

Then there was the Royal Mail inquiry and the subsequent trial in 1931 of the company's chairman, Lord Kylsant. Though now consigned to history, this was the accountancy *cause célèbre* of the inter-war years. Kylsant headed one of the largest British shipping groups of the time, but under him the Royal Mail Steam Packet Co had paid out over seven years dividends worth £5m, while making extensive losses. To pay the dividends the company drew extensively on reserves, and this fact was not revealed, nor did the auditor insist that it should be.

When the truth came out, William McLintock was appointed to report on the company, and from his report sprang the prosecution not only of Lord Kylsant himself, but also of the auditor, HJ Morland, who was senior partner in one of the largest and most respected firms of international accountants. Hence it became a test case for the profession.

Morland was in fact acquitted, but only after the role of the auditor had been put through searching examination and criticism. Kylsant was convicted of issuing a false prospectus and received a sentence of twelve months. The trial lasted nine days, and became a milestone in the development of the modern idea of the function of the auditor as protector of investors' interests.

William McLintock played a prominent part in the trial itself as expert witness and was constantly in the public eye; much work accrued to the firm from this publicity, and he was appointed one of the three trustees who took over the voting rights of the Kylsant Group, thus avoiding a liquidation. The effect of a liquidation of the Royal Mail Group on British exports would have been considerable, so the Treasury and the bankers arranged a moratorium and, since no liquidation took place, audits of these companies had to go on. These were undertaken by William, and for many years the firm was engaged in unravelling the affairs of the Kylsant Group, dealing with the liquidation or re-organization of its various shipping interests. This work continued up till about 1939, and indeed the firm still has on its books a plot of land in West Africa left over from this affair—it is submerged at high tide.

Sir William also became receiver and manager of Gamages, the big London store, when it failed in 1931, and in 1938 chaired a commission of inquiry into the workings of the Northern Ireland Transport Board.

One other interesting development during this period was the setting up of investment trusts; the Grange Trust in 1926 and the Ailsa in 1927. On this occasion William did not display his customary foresight, for these trusts were launched at an inopportune moment and were badly affected by the depression in the early 1930s. The Grange Trust was always administered by the London office; Ailsa was the responsibility of Glasgow. More recently, in accordance with new 'conflict of interest' rules laid down for accountants, management of these trusts has been substantially hived off, although the secretarial work remains.

Just how complete a grip Sir William had on the London office is shown in the deed of partnership of 29 March 1934, which was the foundation of the London office of TMcL as a separate entity from the Glasgow office. The partnership was to commence on 1 April 1934, and the deed was signed by seven partners:

Sir William McLintock
JC Burleigh
John Morison
Charles H McLintock
} Senior partners
T Lister
Duncan McKellar
Thomson McLintock (son of Sir William)

The deed regulated the business carried on from offices situated outside Scotland. In matters concerning policy, conduct, and management of the business, Sir William was to have the final decision.

The capital (clause 5) was to be £50,000 and was to be provided as to £47,500 by the senior partners as Sir William should decide; as to £1,250 by D McKellar and £1,000 by T Lister. The final £250 was to be found by Thomson McLintock.

Sir William was entitled to serve on the board of any company to which he might be appointed a director and any fees were to belong to him. As regards the other partners, any fees paid to them as directors should be dealt with as Sir William directed.

These extracts from the 1934 deed are evidence enough that Sir William was very much the dominating figure. The London office was in fact Sir William, together with his hand-picked associates.

What were the qualities that gave him this dominance? He possessed prodigious energy, as all who worked with him in his prime ruefully acknowledge. He was ruthless in pursuit of his aims and, it must be admitted, was irascible, impatient, and, even at times unreasonable.

During the Royal Mail inquiry and the subsequent trial of Lord Kylsant, Sir William carried a heavy responsibility. There was a body of opinion that felt he had been vindictive in his evidence. Though the Kylsant case brought Sir William very much into the public eye, it also had an adverse effect in some circles and some influential clients removed their business. This was an emotive case, for whole areas of professional standards were brought into the light of public scrutiny and obviously not everyone could be satisfied.

The London office during the period of the Kylsant case worked under great pressure, and Sir William is reported to have been at his most fearsome.

Sir William loved the limelight, was very convivial and a 'born salesman'. For many years he 'held court' at the Savoy Hotel in the Strand which, in effect, became something of a club to him. There was therefore considerable amusement when in 1929, after a hard bargaining session on the London Transport arrangements, Herbert Morrison, the Labour politician, and he went to the Strand about midnight for a meal—and went to a Lyons tea shop. One wonders if the *'bon viveur'* was being diplomatic in the company of a Labour leader. His social activities were certainly pleasurable in themselves; but they also attracted much business. 'During the 20 years, 1919 to 1939, it is estimated that he brought in about 80% of the new work. He worked hard and played hard, burned the candle at both ends and was, in his day, the leading accountant in London,' reports TC Guthrie. An interesting feature of William McLintock's complex personality is the fact that he steadfastly refused all offers of directorships, though he received many. He disliked public speaking and always avoided it if he could; he was never a member of the council of the Glasgow Institute, although he could most certainly have been president. He did, however, help it in less public ways, and several times spoke to its students' societies.

His attitude to international work is also of interest, in view of the firm's later problem in 'going international'. Lord Plender suggested that Deloitte Plender Griffiths and Co, and Thomson McLintock & Co might amalgamate for the purpose of conducting their business in South America. Sir William is reported to have swept the proposal aside, saying, 'It is bad enough men signing my name in Birmingham and Paris but never in Buenos Aires.'

The long list of William McLintock's activities during his heyday in the 1920s and 1930s makes impressive reading. He combined a large private practice with a huge load of work on public bodies and government service. With his gift of attracting the right people to work for him at the right time, he had a fine supporting team in London. Having got good collaborators around him, he had an extraordinary ability to delegate. He was not unreasonable in his demands on his juniors but, having delegated a job, he expected it to be done, even though it might be only a comparatively small part of a vast undertaking. He had no patience with those who wished to run in and out with queries.

Despite his ruthlessness there are many records of Sir William's kindness and friendly approach to all the staff, however humble. Sir Archibald Forbes recollects his advice over living accommodation when as a young man he first moved south from Glasgow. Leslie Bell, who entered the firm in 1921 as an office boy and rose to be senior partner in the tax department, felt he owed his career to the kindness of Sir William who, having heard of Bell's successful efforts in book-keeping studied at night school, gave him the opportunity and encouragement to train as an accountant without the loss of his salary—at that time £25 per annum. He often walked about the office and talked to the staff and was generous and open-handed to those whose work pleased him.

The social side of Sir William's nature came to the fore at staff parties. These were grand occasions with a Scottish flavour, for there were sometimes pipers, a display of sword dancing or reels, and boxes of carnations, white for the ladies and red for the men. At these parties Sir William danced with members of the staff and was always interested in their lives. Following a long-established McLintock tradition, Sir William entertained the staff after the weddings of various members of his family, and took a pride in knowing everyone who worked for him.

Although a man of prodigious energy, Sir William did not enjoy very good health. He suffered from chronic bronchitis and was ill each winter; but it must be remembered that he was sixty in 1933. In 1934, he underwent an operation to remove a kidney, and thereafter did not himself attend the office on Saturdays. Following this operation he developed a new interest; he bought a farm in Norfolk and became extremely involved in it. By 1935 he had distinctly mellowed and was beginning to relax his grip on the firm.

From his youth he had always enjoyed sport and as a boy and young man was a keen tennis player. In later life he played golf (his handicap was four) and regularly went to

Cruden Bay for a month's golfing holiday. In later years he also became an enthusiastic shot. Each winter he spent a month in the south of France but this was probably associated with his bronchitis and the need to get away from London in foggy weather. He was a good looking man, always impeccably dressed.

Sir William was a remarkable man with great foresight and drive. His reputation for fearsomeness probably derived in part from his high standard of efficiency and in part from his insistence on having his own way and being the central figure. But his greatest skill seems to have lain in his ability to choose the right men to work with him, and then to delegate to them and subsequently master the brief provided and assimilate the facts in it quickly and accurately.

Chapter Four

GLASGOW CONSOLIDATED: THE INTER-WAR YEARS

THE GLASGOW firm may sometimes seem to have been swamped by the rapid growth of the London firm and over-shadowed by the personality of Sir William McLintock. But the plain fact was that the big business in the inter-war years lay in the south, and was simply not there to be had in Scotland. As a consequence, the staff of the Glasgow firm remained at a fairly constant figure, unlike the explosive growth of London, and the financial figures tell much the same story.

But if this was a period when business in Glasgow was on a plateau, nevertheless several important gains were made. Not the least of these was that McLintocks consolidated its reputation and position so as to become in due course what many regarded as the leading firm of accountants in the west of Scotland, and probably just about the largest single firm in the whole of Scotland. This, as we shall see, was to have important consequences later when the rush of mergers transformed the accountancy scene in Scotland during the 1960s.

Again, the formal separation into two firms in 1934 was in many ways advantageous to Glasgow. Prior to that Sir William McLintock had in effect operated a 'brain-drain' and persuaded many of the most able staff to go south. After 1934, Glasgow settled down to its own business.

The Glasgow firm also had, and has, several assets which give it great strength. It is, in effect, the original firm, occupying the same premises at 216 West George Street, which it has occupied without interruption since 1918. A lease was taken on 203 West George Street from 30 September 1936 to Whit Sunday 1940, and 212 West George Street was bought in November 1939. There is an old-fashioned charm and friendly neighbourliness about the West George Street office which it would be impossible to replace. The old private houses have been skilfully converted and kept up-to-date.

But the dark woodwork and polished brass of the staircases and the dignified portraits of former senior partners in the boardroom (not to mention the TMcL monogram carved into the banisters leading up from the entrance hall) preserve an air of dignity and tradition that the spanking new London office, for all its comparative luxury, cannot compete with. The fact that the freeholds in West George Street are owned by the firm has also proved of great value in keeping down costs—another instance of the prudent laying of foundations in the otherwise rather uneventful inter-war period.

The hundreds of CAs who have graduated in the Glasgow office, and many of whom now occupy senior positions in industry and commerce worldwide, constitute another aspect of the 'assets' of that office. None of them, it should be said, would feel that this history had been adequately written if the record did not, as it now does, include mention of Robert Hay. Robert, whose job title was 'cashier', was in reality mentor, friend, setter of rigorous standards, focus for a thousand reminiscences. He commanded the employee area of the firm for well nigh forty years and his memory is embedded in all that 216 West George Street means to so many of its alumni.

Another lasting asset of Glasgow has been that the pace of life is less severe than in London—travel, services and amenities generally are better and the quick access to really open country or to the sea are matters to be envied by anyone tied to an office in London. A young man in West George Street can keep old clothes in the office and climb Ben Lomond after work or go off on a long bicycle ride through the neighbouring hills in the evening. Obviously, it is just as easy to play a round of golf, go sailing, go fishing or indulge in numerous other activities at a time of day when less fortunate mortals in the south are condemned to traffic jams or long, over-crowded train journeys.

This is not to imply that life was leisurely in Glasgow between the wars. A wide range of business was carried out, including audit, taxation, coal industry work, insurance, factoring, investigations, secretarial and liquidations.

The new dispensation in Glasgow, free from the London office, was inaugurated by the signing of a new contract of copartnery, dated 28/29 March 1934 but taking effect from 1 April 1930. The partners were:

Sir William McLintock TL McLintock J Duncan	Senior partners
W Anderson	
JT Dowling	
HE Borland	
TC Currie	
JH Haddow	

It was laid down that the business in Scotland should be treated as entirely separate from that carried on outside Scotland. Furthermore, no party was to be interested in business carried on outside Scotland other than Sir William. The goodwill and the right to the name of Thomson McLintock & Co in Scotland was to vest in the three senior partners.

In fact, it would appear from documents held in the London and Glasgow offices that some moves were made in London as early as 1927 to revise the partnership deed. In the Glasgow records there is an unsigned agreement, not dated but purporting to run from 1 April 1927 to 31 March 1931, which altered the percentage of profits due to the respective partners named in the draft. This document is marked in pencil 'not proceeded with'; but the accounts make it apparent that the division of profits was thereafter made in accordance with the draft.

Despite the fact that there is no other evidence of the discussions or problems of the parent and offspring of Thomson McLintock & Co during these years, it may fairly be surmised that the complete separation in 1934 resulted only after many tergiversations. The position must have been that Sir William McLintock was quite clear that he was going to control the London office as he considered fit. As a 'subsidiary' of the Glasgow firm, this could not easily be arranged since his half-brother, TL McLintock, and John Duncan were scarcely likely to be willing to play merely subservient roles. The separation of the accounts and the division of profits from 1931 was therefore a *de facto* separation of the partnership which was later given legal effect in 1934 in Glasgow and London.

But a compromise was reached insofar as Sir William, while senior partner in London, remained one of the senior partners in Glasgow.

This arrangement—separate partnerships with separate accounts and profits but retaining a common partner as the link—was an interesting and fairly exact precedent for the federal system that McLintocks was later to adopt in its national and international expansion in the 1960s and 1970s. But it is not at all clear what the real influence of Sir William was on the Glasgow firm from 1934. His status was probably that of an adviser whilst the essential business was carried on by the other two senior partners.

In particular, the character and policy of the Glasgow firm between the wars must be related to the character of its senior partner for most of that period, Thomson Liddell McLintock, eldest son of Thomson McLintock's second marriage. He was as different from his ambitious worldly half-brother as it was possible to be.

TL McLintock was born on 21 June 1879, and was thus almost six years younger than his half-brother. He was educated at Dumfries Academy and later at Glasgow High School and subsequently trained in the family firm, qualifying as a chartered accountant in 1900. He spent his whole working life in the Glasgow office and for very many years attended to all the practical, administrative aspects of the business.

At first impression Mr TL, as he was always referred to, seems a dull and even insignificant figure. He inherited to the full his father's high principles and upright character. He was a non-smoker, strict teetotaller and a stickler for punctuality — all qualities which were used in his administrative role in the Glasgow office. Those who smoked or liked to drink, such as the odd character McKim already referred to, kept well out of his way. Andrew Black, in his notes on the firm, gave this picture of him: 'Mr TL sat in a small office with a clear glass window overlooking the general office. Smoking and tea-drinking in offices were then unknown and Mr TL was very strict about smoking; even when about to leave the office anyone found lighting a cigarette before he was outside the office would hear about it. At the Glasgow office parties no alcohol was allowed and care had to be taken that the fruit cup served to TL and his party should be innocuous whilst lesser mortals saw to it that theirs was well-laced.'

TL was both a very withdrawn person—until, that is, you got to know him very well indeed — and also financially well off in his own right, as was his wife. He therefore felt no great urge to be adventurous or ambitious, nor indeed was he temperamentally suited to be so. He was, however, very much the boss, very conscious that he bore the firm's name, and he rarely consulted others. To the end of his life an appointment with TL was conducted with ceremony; he was well-protected by an efficient secretary and under no circumstances did anyone, client, partner or apprentice make contact with him unless the ritual was followed. On the other hand, he was extremely scrupulous about how he attracted business. He was a sound accountant and inherited from his father a number of important clients, which he kept.

This picture of a rather austere and narrow man is,

however, by no means the whole story. TL from his early childhood showed, like his father and half-brother before him, marked musical talent; the invaluable private ledger contains numerous entries: 'Tom's violin' and reference to singing lessons. In later life he is even reputed to have played the banjo, odd as it sounds in view of his character. He is remembered as a courtly person with a distinguished presence, well capable of being kindly and generous but much identified with Thomson McLintock's more puritan side; a very different character not only from his flamboyant half-brother but also from his lively younger brother, Charles.

With the increasing pre-occupation of William McLintock with the affairs of the London business, culminating in his removal south in 1917, TL McLintock took administrative charge of the Glasgow office. He obviously disliked change and endeavoured to run it, even after his father's death in 1920, on what might be termed old-fashioned methods. He must have had considerable strength of character, for he withstood many broadsides from London during the 1920s. The strict side of his character can also be illustrated by the fact that after the 1914–1918 war, when faced with a generation of ex-servicemen, many of whom were older and somewhat unruly as compared to the apprentices of pre-war days, he installed a time clock in the office. Everyone, except partners, was expected to clock in morning and evening and also at lunchtime.

Indeed, they were supposed to do so whenever they left the office on an errand, but this was usually circumvented! In spite of derisory comments by rival firms about 'McLintock's factory', TL had his way and the clock remained until it was removed 'for a trial period' about 1950. It was never re-introduced, though the clock is said to be still lurking in the attics of 216 West George Street.

TL McLintock was therefore in his own way a most interesting man. He probably regarded William McLintock's activities and meteoric rise with a kindly humour but remained well satisfied in his comparatively humdrum role in

Glasgow, where he was able to dominate the partnership. Right from childhood, when the two boys spent much time together, TL stood out for his ability not to be overshadowed by his half-brother – in the circumstances, no mean feat.

Chapter Five

THE WAR YEARS: 1939–1945

London

SIR WILLIAM MCLINTOCK, with his customary mixture of foresight and self-interest, had made arrangements for emergency offices in part of the Froebel Institute in Roehampton Lane, on the edge of London. These were occupied on the outbreak of war, in September 1939, while some partners and staff carried on at Oxford Court and Granite House, both in Cannon Street. The emergency offices were convenient for Sir William himself, since he lived in Wimbledon; but they were not particularly safe or free from bombing. The Thames, with its bridges, was too near and the river was always a useful guide for enemy bombers. Lack of public transport in the district and the inevitable chaos of the blitz made it even less convenient for many members of the staff. There are numerous recollections of the long walk down Roehampton Lane, of the use of bicycles, of lodgings taken in the neighbourhood and of Sir William's concern that members of his staff should be given lifts in his car as often as possible.

On 3 September 1939 the young men in the audit room dug a trench in the grounds of the Froebel Institute. As the books were brought down from the Oxford Court offices they were placed in the trench and subsequently were taken there every evening for safety. The trench served as an air-raid shelter in the early part of the war and, on one occasion when the premises were machine-gunned, the staff took cover in it. At a later stage a more substantial shelter was constructed in the stable buildings.

In May 1941 Oxford Court was destroyed and Granite House was severely damaged in the blitz. It is possible that Oxford Court might have been saved, for the fire which came from next door did not spread to that building until 6 am. However, there was no water available to control the flames. Not only were the water mains broken but, by ill-chance, there was an extremely low tide at the time and the firemen's hoses could not reach the river water in the Thames. On the night the offices were bombed, JC Burleigh was the partner on fire-watching duty. He and the other members of the team worked throughout that night and all the next day rescuing documents and papers. The water from the firemen's hoses caused the usual appalling mess and even late in the afternoon it proved difficult and dangerous to salvage papers from the metal safes in the basement, for the water down there was scalding hot and several of the men were badly burnt as they worked. The rescued deed boxes and files were taken out to Roehampton and eye-witnesses recall the dreadful smell of the papers when the boxes were opened.

During the war a considerable quantity of Treasury notes were held in the office for emergency use. When the box containing these notes was opened, they had all turned to ashes. Fortunately, the serial numbers were recorded and the Bank of England replaced them. In spite of the bombing the City office was operating again from Granite House within a week and continued to do so throughout the rest of the war.

At Roehampton the staff were organized into groups of fire-watchers, each group consisting of a partner, two men and two women working on a rota system. Camp beds and food were provided and Sir William lent his portable wireless to those on duty; but this had to be put back in his office each morning. On one occasion the wireless had not been turned off properly and at mid-morning it blared forth 'Workers' Playtime' or something similar to the astonishment and fury of Sir William.

A first aid squad was formed under the leadership of Miss Robertson, Sir William's personal secretary, which was joined by many members of the staff. Miss Robertson also organized a war comforts scheme and parcels were sent to all members of the staff serving in the forces.

There were many expedients for alleviating the shortages of those days. JC Burleigh was a very keen gardener and had an allotment in the grounds of the Froebel Institue. He distributed the produce among his staff. Charles McLintock kept goats at his home in Surrey and frequently brought milk up to be shared around. Sir William himself brought produce from his Norfolk farm and he also sent many war-weary members of the staff to Norfolk for a well-earned rest. Many members of the staff were in the forces or engaged in war work, though Sir William never let any one go if he could persuade him otherwise, for he felt that Thomson McLintock & Co were making their contribution to the war effort in their own field. Nevertheless, there were staff shortages and those remaining worked long hours.

Other difficulties cropped up, for clothing became difficult to get and was rationed. Stockings, in particular, were very hard to find and in summertime typists came to the office with bare legs. This met with severe disapproval from Sir William and he even objected to staff coming to work without hats.

But, whatever the difficulties, work had to go on. Though no longer young, and in failing health, Sir William saw to it that his staff did not falter. He did all he could for their comfort and safety—and then expected them to get the job done.

There were problems too in the partnership. By an agreement dated 19 January 1942, Thomson McLintock junior, Sir William's son, retired as from 31 March 1941. Clearly, he had not been a success. By an agreement dated only two days later, 21 January 1942, John Kissane also retired from the partnership. Sir William and Kissane are reputed to have had incompatible temperaments; this event would certainly indicate such, since men of Kissane's qualifications were hard to obtain during the war years.

By 1946 Sir William was a sick man and did not sign the accounts for that year; he died in May 1947, and the accounts for 1947 were signed by his executors. Charles McLintock, likewise, did not sign the 1946 accounts and died in January 1947. Thus both faded from the partnership at the same time and the McLintock name disappeared from the London partnership until Alan McLintock, the son of Charles, became a partner in 1954. In Glasgow there was a shorter hiatus – T Ian McLintock, son of TL McLintock, became a partner there in 1949, and retired through ill-health in 1965. But, for London, the passing of both William and Charles McLintock, so soon after the end of the war, clearly marked the close of an era.

Glasgow

A vivid picture of the war years in Glasgow has been provided by TC Currie. Emergency premises were taken in a private house at Anniesland, an outer suburb of Glasgow, which was used as a store for important papers and copies of documents. The partners took copies of papers to their homes; for example, Currie 'took all the taxation computation copies to Troon each day along with any other important items or at least items which seemed at the time to be important'. An air-raid shelter was created in the basement of the office and fully equipped; a grant of £200 was made towards the cost of it.

An amusing side-light was the marked hierarchy in ARP curtains. J Duncan's room had 'one pair green serge window curtains' though his ante-room had only 'pair ARP black Italian cloth curtains'. Partners' rooms had 'ARP green cloth curtains' and all general offices, typing room etc black Italian cloth.

Glasgow fortunately escaped severe bombing apart from the Clydebank raids in 1941. TC Currie, and no doubt many other members of the staff, spent a night on the office roof at that time. After these raids an emergency bed was kept in John Duncan's room where it remained for many years.

A glimpse of the staff shortage can be obtained from the fact that Jim Dowling's sister, Kathleen Dowling, appeared on the pay-roll from September 1939 until December 1942. No doubt she was not the only person closely associated with a partner or member of the staff who was brought in to help.

In the Glasgow partnership, the biggest change came in 1940 when TL McLintock died and John Duncan took over as senior partner, a position he was to hold for twenty years. Duncan had been an important figure in the Glasgow partnership for many years. Born in 1882 and educated at Lenzie Academy he passed his final examination (with distinction) in 1904, was admitted as a member of the Institute of Accountants and Actuaries in 1905 and, in the same year, joined the staff of Thomson McLintock & Co. He became a close friend of William McLintock, but in 1909 left McLintocks and became a member of the firm of Chrystal, Irvine and Duncan, CA, Glasgow. For in 1909 Charles, the youngest of the McLintock brothers, was an apprentice and it was intended that he should be made a partner when he qualified; there was therefore no opportunity for Duncan in the partnership at that time. In fact, events did not develop as anticipated and he re-joined the firm in 1916. He was made a junior partner and remained with the firm until his death in February 1960.

When he re-entered the firm he brought with him a large staff and had a position of special importance from the beginning. After Thomson McLintock died in 1920 the Glasgow office was under the charge of TL McLintock, with Duncan as second-in-command. Then in 1934, when the firm divided, TL McLintock remained senior partner in Glasgow but both he and Sir William in London were at liberty to choose how much time they devoted to the business. Duncan had no such choice and became, in effect, working senior partner in Glasgow, six years before becoming actual senior partner.

Perhaps John Duncan's chief contribution was in the field of education. He was greatly interested in the welfare and progress of apprentices and in his early years was a popular and effective tutor. He served on the General Examining Board of the Chartered Accountants of Scotland from 1920 to 1928, and was a member of the council of the Glasgow Institute from 1917 to 1920 and from 1942 to 1945. He also served on the joint committee of the councils of the three Scottish chartered accountancy bodies from 1944 to 1948. In 1946, he was elected president of the Institute of Accountants and Actuaries in Glasgow.

During the years when he was involved directly with training, Duncan was well placed to pick out promising students. One of these was JC Burleigh, who joined the London firm after the first world war, and another was Jim Dowling, both of whom had long and successful careers with the firm and became senior partners in London and in Glasgow respectively. Dowling always warmly acknowledged the fact that 'He was given his chance by John Duncan'.

In addition, Duncan did much benevolent work. He was president of the Scottish Chartered Accountants Benevolent Association, 1948 to 1949, and served on the executive committee from 1951 to 1956. He also took part in the local church and benevolent work in his native Lenzie.

Duncan always had a great admiration for Sir William McLintock and although they obviously had 'many a bonny fight' in the years immediately preceding 1934 they remained firm friends. Duncan always attended functions in the London office, the weddings of Sir William's children and similar events, and on many occasions was invited to speak. He was, like so many other McLintock men in Glasgow, a good golfer, but also liked shooting and curling.

He had a wide range of business activities, held many important audit and other professional appointments, and in addition he served on the board of several commercial concerns and investment trust companies. He is remembered as a particularly friendly man, generous, unaffected and frank, who could bring a certain gaiety to a rather dry profession. 'He was that somewhat rare thing—a man who was both popular and gifted', said the *Glasgow Herald* on his death.

Chapter Six

INTERREGNUM TO RECONCILIATION: 1946–1959

WHEN SIR WILLIAM died in May 1947, the great figure of the London firm disappeared, and JC Burleigh took over the controls as senior partner. It must have been a very difficult task to establish a new pattern after years of one-man rule, an autocracy which had established the firm among the leading accountants of the country. One thing, however, was clear; there never should be one single controlling partner again. The period following Sir William's death may be regarded as confirming the London firm in the position it had attained, rather than as breaking much new ground. No single new star appeared, partly deliberately, and partly because the time had passed when that was the normal way of running big organizations.

After August 1945 the Roehampton office had been relinquished and the firm, while remaining at Granite House, took additional office space in Surrey Street, Strand. In December 1948 Granite House was given up in favour of the new office at King William Street; the offices in Surrey Street were only abandoned in September 1949, when all the staff were finally housed under one roof at King William Street.

The characters of the senior partners in London at that time fitted the character of the period—or perhaps were partly responsible for it. JC Burleigh, who took over from 1947 to 1954, was a shy quiet person, not well-known outside his own office, and had for many years lived under the shadow of Sir William.

He was one of the many Scotsmen who joined the London firm. After passing the final examination with distinction, he was admitted to membership of the Institute of Accountants and Actuaries in Glasgow in 1912, and shortly after took up a commercial appointment in London. He was therefore never in the Glasgow office of Thomson McLintock, but was introduced to William McLintock by John Duncan. On the outbreak of war in 1914, he was commissioned and served for nearly four years in France. Demobilized in May 1919, he joined the London office of McLintocks immediately, was admitted to partnership in 1920 and became one of those hand-picked, extremely able collaborators, who formed the early London team. He led an exceptionally strenuous professional life, devoting a great deal of his time and energy to his work. It might be said that Burleigh was the most 'general' partner ever to have been in the firm, for he undertook a great variety of work. His sphere of interest encompassed audit work, taxation, liquidation and a remarkable degree of personal interest in the affairs of clients. During the 1939–1945 war, he dealt with the affairs of various exiled European monarchs.

Rather late in life he married the daughter of a colleague, FJ Cooksey, the tax expert, and found relaxation in family life, tennis and gardening, at which be became adept; in short, a superb accountant, but not an adventurous man.

His successor as senior partner in London, from 1954 to 1958, was in many ways a very similar man. Sir John Morison was also a quiet and unassuming person who hated ostentation in any form and shunned the 'bright lights', while being a man of outstanding intellectual ability, with great skill in negotiation and an enormous capacity for work.

He was a native of Greenock, educated at Greenock Academy and apprenticed to Thomson McLintock & Co, Glasgow. There is a revealing story about the young Morison and William McLintock. During the first world war Morison joined the army and was wounded; he was sent back to England and spent a considerable period in a military hospital

216 West George Street – Glasgow office since 1918

T. McL

					£	s	d
1880				£50-2-1	38	16	6
Feb	25	To	Self		1		
	27		Hat (Cloth)	40-3--		6	6
Mch	2		Re-gilding Teapot			10	
	3		R Robertsons Wife		1		
			Self			4	
	4		House		7	10	
			Present for J Moris		1	6	
			Self		1		
	5		Marriage present for Agnes ..		1	13	6
	8		Insurance Premium Norwich Union		3	9	
	10		Payments to Building Society		20		
			Dressed Hat & Tam o'Shanter			17	
	12		House Gas A/c		1	14	2
			James White		1	11	6
			E. Bydewell			11	10
	13		Self		2		
	16		Self		1		
	19		Insurance Premium		1	6	9
			Monogram			7	6
			Self Dinner Set &c		3		
	20		House		7	10	
				£90-5-1	56	11	3

3.

T. McL

					£	s	d
1880				90-5-1	56	11	3
Mch	24	To	C. Robertson Rent	57.12.3	1	1	
Apl	3	To	House		7	10	
		"	Wm Smith S. S.			7	7
		"	Loan of M. L. Slides S. Brown			17	6
	5	"	Carriage of Golden Texts			2	
		"	Self		1		
	7	"	Hat			6	
		"	Self		2		
	15	"	House		7	10	
	17	"	Self		1	10	
		"	Loan of Slides			2	6
	22	"	Self		2		
	24	"	Self		1		
		"	Insurance Premium Reliance	29.6.3	5	8	
May	2	To	Cash		5		
	5	"	"		1		
	8	"	"		1		
	11	"	Stewart's A/c		13		
	14	"	House		15		
	15	"	Rent of House		14	12	6
	19	"	Botanic Gardens Ticket		1	1	
				177.3.7	50	13	[illegible]

A PERSONAL CASH ACCOUNT – 1880

West George Street in 1920

[*Glasgow Heral*

in London. William McLintock, knowing of his whereabouts, requested the War Office to release him for work in the London office. After considerable argument, it was agreed that Morison could leave hospital daily, provided he wore his hospital blue uniform. He was, of course, by no means fit, certainly not to work at William McLintock's accustomed pace. On one occasion, he passed out while working late in William McLintock's flat. When he came to he found himself lying on a bed with his collar and tie loosened and a few rugs covering him. William McLintock must have carried him there, made him comfortable, and returned to his task, for when Morison tottered into the other room—the time being about 6 am—William McLintock was still at the table working as he had been throughout the night.

Morison passed the final examination, also with distinction, and was admitted to the Institute of Accountants and Actuaries in Glasgow in 1920. He joined the partnership of Thomson McLintock & Co, Glasgow, in January 1920, but here was a man after Sir William's own heart and Sir William was clearly determined that Morison should move to London. He brought with him from Glasgow his personal secretary, Miss Love, who worked with him for some thirty-five years. Morison was thus another of that hand-picked group who worked under Sir William.

During the second world war Morison was seconded to the Ministry of Supply for three years and was also on the War Damage Commission and similar bodies. For these services he received a knighthood in 1945. Later, he played a leading part in drawing up the plan for the de-nationalization of the steel industry by the Conservative government of the early 1950s; subsequently he became chairman of the Iron and Steel Holding and Realization Agency formed to put the plan into effect. For these services he was appointed GBE. In spite of thirty-two years' residence in London, Morison's heart remained in Scotland and he was never happier than on his annual holiday to Lochranza in the Isle of Arran, where, during the month of September, he could relax and play his own modest game of golf on the local course.

He died 'in harness' in March 1958. Two of his sons, Robert and Arthur, followed him into the firm and both, like their father, passed the Scottish chartered accountants' final examination with distinction, thus creating a family record which is believed to be unique. Both are key figures in the London partnership today.

It was not until the arrival of Thomas Lister as senior partner in London from 1958 to 1967 that the evolution of the firm was once again resumed. Although very much a William McLintock man like his two predecessors, Lister was an unusual man who in his career more than once broke new ground. Educated at the Royal High School, Edinburgh, and at Edinburgh University, he was apprenticed to Messrs A & J Robertson CA, Edinburgh (now a part of the TMcL family in Scotland) and was admitted to membership of the Society of Accountants in Edinburgh in 1915, having obtained distinction in his final examination. After serving in the first world war from 1915 to 1919, he took up an industrial appointment for a short time, then in 1921 joined the staff of Thomson McLintock & Co, London, becoming a partner in 1931.

Lister possessed a keen analytical mind and was an accountant of outstanding ability, having an enthusiasm, somewhat rare in the profession, for actuarial science. He was also a deeply religious man and much interested in temperance work. As an early member of Sir William's London team, with his precise and academic outlook, he was the ideal person to set up the machine and make the system work. For all that, he had a nice sense of humour about his work, as befitted a lover of Gilbert and Sullivan operas.

In addition to direct involvement in the business of Thomson McLintock & Co, he undertook much outside work. For example, he was a member of the Spens Committee, which reported on the remuneration for doctors and dentists under the National Health Service, and was on a number of other government committees.

Lister always took a keen interest in the affairs of the Institute of Chartered Accountants of Scotland, and was chairman of the Association of Scottish Chartered Accountants in London and also convener of a committee, always referred to as 'the Lister Committee', appointed by the council to review the examination and training of apprentices. That committee's recommendations resulted in important changes in the training of accountants in Scotland, including the introduction of an academic year spent in university study. In 1959, in spite of the fact that he practised in London, he was accorded the honour of being elected president of the Institute of Chartered Accountants of Scotland—the first from outside Scotland. As well as being a personal honour to Lister, this appointment also recognized the importance to the Institute of the large number of its members—nearly 1,900—then resident south of the border.

But his greatest single service to TMcL was undoubtedly his piloting of the reunion, after many years of *de facto* separation, of the London and Glasgow offices. This was clearly the first priority in his mind when he took over as senior partner, and was greatly eased by his personal friendship with his opposite number in Glasgow, James Dowling. At a partners' meeting in London on 26 January 1959, it was recorded that 'views had been expressed that the present indeterminate association with Glasgow, whilst it had worked perfectly well in the past, was not satisfactory as a permanent arrangement. It might prove even less satisfactory as time went on and as the close personal links, created between the individual partners in the earlier years of the two firms when their businesses were closely connected, were broken. . . .

'To establish a more definite association . . . the two firms would walk in step and would not unknowingly have major differences of policy . . . it was decided to suggest to Glasgow that the senior partner of each office should be a partner in the other, having no substantial interest in the profits but having a right to take part in discussions on all important questions of policy or principle. One firm, for instance, would not seek to introduce a new partner without consulting the representative of the other.

'. . . Since the earlier discussions, the matter had been mentioned informally to Mr Dowling (because of Mr Duncan's health it was thought that he should not be expected to be the partner to join the London firm). It was agreed that Mr Lister should go ahead with the matter and write to Mr Dowling putting forward specific suggestions.'

Lister duly wrote to Dowling on 27 January 1959, and the new arrangement was agreed upon.

So it came about that the (or a) senior partner in each office should become a partner in the other, without putting up capital or sharing profits. This echoed the arrangement of the Glasgow office with Sir William McLintock in the 1930s, but, more important, set the pattern, perhaps once and for all, for the whole subsequent development of the firm in extending its national and international coverage. What is more, the reunion of London and Glasgow was an essential first step in this development process, without which little else could have been done. It was therefore an historic move for the firm, for which great credit must be given both to Lister and to the remarkable figure who co-piloted the reunion from Glasgow, James Dowling.

Dowling joined McLintocks in Glasgow as an apprentice in 1919 after leaving Glasgow Academy, and remained with the firm throughout his working life of almost fifty years. He became an important and much sought after accountant in Scotland, and one of the foremost members of the accounting profession in Great Britain. He was admitted to membership of the Institute of Accountants and Actuaries in Glasgow in 1925 and became a partner in McLintocks in 1931 at the early age of twenty-nine. He in effect ran the Glasgow office for some years before becoming formally the senior partner on the death of John Duncan in February 1960, and held this office for nine busy and highly effective years. During this period the link with London was, as we have seen, re-forged, management accounting was developed, and the overseas involvement established. Dowling retired in March 1969, though 'retirement' for him was a relative term; he retained a number of personal appointments and remained active until his sudden death in November 1972.

For many years he was, like so many other McLintock men, much involved in the affairs of The Institute of Chartered Accountants of Scotland. After his admission to membership in 1925 he coached for the Institute's examinations; later he became president of the Glasgow Chartered Accountants Students' Society and a member of the General Examining Board. He was appointed to the Council in 1955 and became president of the Institute in 1957 to 1958. He was distinguished by being awarded an honorary J Dip MA on the inception of that higher degree in management accounting. He made a considerable contribution to the policy of the Institute, regularly attended the summer school and was a staunch supporter of the various social activities, where he was much in demand as an entertaining speaker.

Dowling's particular interest in training probably stemmed from his own student days. He used to recall the excruciating boredom of his first two years, which for him had been scarcely endurable. He often regretted that he did not in fact train as an actuary, an interest which he shared with his friend Tom Lister. In his early years he was frequently in receipt of bonus payments for special work and for many years he was recognized as the natural successor to John Duncan. He must have been regarded by Sir William as the lynch-pin of the Glasgow firm, for when, in 1940, his friend Sir Archibald Forbes urged him to join him in work for the Air Ministry (later the Ministry of Aircraft Production), Sir William telephoned Forbes in great wrath: 'Have you no loyalty? Do you want to ruin your old firm?' In vain did Sir Archibald plead the greater peril facing the whole country at that time. There is no record of what transpired subsequently between Sir William and Dowling; but Jim stayed in Glasgow and, with the failing health and increasing age of

John Duncan, more and more responsibility devolved on to him. There were other opportunities to enter the business world where, without doubt, he would have risen to eminence. These offers were refused and the Glasgow firm was the richer for it.

'He was a supremely good practitioner—absolutely sound, quick to get to the heart of a problem, and to propose a constructive solution. He had a gift of clear exposition, both orally and in writing. And he had also the gift of inspiring those who worked with him, so that his standards became theirs. . . . But shining through his professional skill and giving it an extra dimension was another quality—his warm humanity. It was this quality which brought him affection as well as respect. He liked people, and they returned his liking in the fullest measure.

'Although he worked so hard, he seemed always to have unlimited time to listen sympathetically, and, having listened, to give sound advice. He was a natural confidant. The many who asked him for advice on professional or personal problems—and he did not broadcast advice unasked—knew that their confidences were safe with him. When he had to criticize, he did so gently and understandingly.' So wrote *The Accountants' Magazine* on his death. He was a modest man and had the great attribute of a lively sense of humour. His humour may be illustrated by a story which he liked to tell. Early in his career he was summoned to take a cheque, for a very large sum of money (in fact, many millions), to the bank. He described how his eyes popped out of his head at all the noughts—he had never seen such a sum written out—and how he ran down West George Street with the precious cheque clasped to his chest. He also liked to maintain a fiction that his father had kept a 'sweetie shop', conjuring up the picture of a simple establishment where children spent their pocket money. In fact the business was in high quality confectionery.

He held numerous business appointments including directorships of the Bank of Scotland and of several investment trusts. Shortly before his death he was appointed vice-president of the Scottish Amicable Life Assurance Society. In 1953, he became a member of the Board of Referees and a trustee of the Scottish Hospital Endowments Research Trust. His advice was sought in a wide variety of industrial inquiries. He was a member of numerous committees, particularly those set up by the Scottish Council (Development and Industry), one of which led to the resuscitation of the Scottish slate industry after the war. In 1950, he was a member of the committee set up to inquire into the problems of the Aberdeen fishing industry.

It is remarkable that such a busy man also had time to devote to charitable work; but, for many years, he was associated with Quarriers' Homes, of which he was at the time of his death honorary treasurer. In addition he was appointed a Justice of the Peace for the County of the City of Glasgow in 1967.

For relaxation he was a keen fisherman, escaping to a small loch near Glasgow whenever pressure of work allowed, and annually taking a beat on the Spey. There he and a group of close friends pursued salmon with all the chances of that particular sport. Nor did he neglect golf, having earlier been a keen tennis player.

Jim Dowling became an eminent, much loved and respected man in his own land. The enigma of his life lies perhaps in his refusal to be attracted away from his native heath to the greater, or, one should rather say, the more obvious worldly rewards which could so easily have been his. No doubt his decision was a wise one, carefully weighed and balanced. It seems incredible that when he became engaged, his fiancée, Jean, was asked, 'What do you want to marry Jim Dowling for? He'll not make anything.'

What he 'made', along with his friend Tom Lister, was the transition of Thomson McLintock & Co into the modern era of competitive international business, as it stands at the time of the firm's centenary. The two men are therefore 'watershed' figures in McLintocks' history, and with them we fittingly close Part One of its narration, and cross to Part Two.

PART II

Chapter Seven

THE PHILOSOPHY OF EXPANSION

THE 'REMARRIAGE' of the Glasgow and London offices in 1959 set in train the development of Thomson McLintock into the modern firm of today. In that development, a number of main themes emerged, interacting with each other and with the character of the people who were responsible for them. The first, and in many eyes the most important, of these themes was the growth of the international organization, beginning with an abortive move into Canada, which, however, established transatlantic connections which later blossomed into what is now the international firm of McLintock Main Lafrentz. While still not a money-maker in its own right, the real question is rather how much business McLintocks and Main Lafrentz between them would have lost if they had not been able to develop this new dimension.

The second main theme is the increasing size and complexity of the business. The size of the audit jobs has got bigger, the size of the firm and its staff has got bigger, and the complexity of the work has increased, as shown particularly in the development of computer auditing and in the consortium that was set up with two other firms of accountants to deal with both the computer facility and management accounting; that consortium is now in the course of being phased out.

Thirdly, there has been the continued development of the taxation practice, long a strength of the firm, but now more than ever a vital dimension. On the personal tax side, there has been continuing demand for the service.

Fourthly, there has been the sheer physical growth of the firm, organic growth supplemented by alliances formed with major out-of-London or out-of-Glasgow firms. The only outright merger in London has been with Martin Farlow, and that arose mainly out of the development of the international side; in Glasgow, the only outright merger was with Robertson & Maxtone Graham in 1975. Since the forties and fifties when, in addition to London (then the biggest office) and Glasgow (the oldest), there were still only the Birmingham and Manchester offices, the need has grown for a McLintock presence in most of the major cities of the country, both to service London-based clients, and to generate a bigger flow of business in and from the provinces. Partly thanks to the abolition of legal restrictions on partnerships in the late 1960s, there has therefore been a rapid development in national coverage, with the activity particularly marked between 1963 and 1970, and then again in 1974/75. But at least as important as the pace and direction of this expansion, national and international, was the manner and philosophy with which it was done, and this forms a separate and fifth theme on its own. The style and shape of MML, the international organization, will be discussed in a later chapter, as will the very important and sixth post-war theme of training people to suit the modern needs of the firm.

The distinctive feature of the TMcL philosophy is the idea of the 'federation', a deliberately decentralized organization in which very substantial powers of autonomy are left in the hands of the local partners of each regional firm. Of course, the London and Glasgow offices are bound, separately and together, to exercise enormous influence over the whole, both because of their size and because they are the original centres of TMcL. But that has not been allowed to develop, as it might in other circumstances have done, into a highly centralized institution in which all orders flow down from the centre to the principal parts. Other accountancy firms have of course chosen that route, and there is no general rule; it is really a question of what is suitable and possible for a particular firm at a particular time. In the case of TMcL, the theoretical alternative of opening its own branches, with sufficient resources to expand under their own momentum, was out of the question; TMcL simply did not have the financial strength to adopt that approach. Indeed, one problem that faced the firm was that some of the small branch offices which it did establish (and in some cases still has) were simply not big enough to become the basis for expansion. This has inevitably led to a search for established local firms who would be willing and suitable to come under the TMcL banner.

It is, however, also fair to say that other national firms of accountants have expanded in a similar way, by absorbing local firms, but have not adopted the 'federal' idea at all, but fitted the new acquisitions into a centralized structure. So there were certainly further reasons for TMcL adopting that idea, and they lie partly in the temperament and outlook of the partners of the original London and Glasgow offices, and partly in the temperament and outlook of the firms taken over. For on the one side there was little desire to run a centralized institution, especially as, by an accident of historical circumstances, TMcL was already 'decentralized' between two main offices, London and Glasgow, neither of which was likely to yield supremacy to the other; and on the other side, many of the firms which have joined McLintocks would not have done so unless they were assured of continuing scope and authority within the overall framework of the firm.

It is instructive to compare TMcL in this respect with another successful firm of accountants, which in many other ways bears a remarkable similarity to TMcL. This particular firm of accountants was founded about the turn of the century; as late as 1960 it was still a small firm with twelve partners. Then it embarked, late in the day as did McLintocks, on expansion; it also was too small to set up its own offices everywhere with any hope of success, and went for a policy of merging with established local firms, as did TMcL. But in the UK it now has a single managing partner, rather like the managing director of a company, and a board which makes binding decisions for the whole partnership; all profits are pooled. That, then, is a highly centralized system, as unlike TMcL as could be, yet starting from a not dissimilar position.

The 'federal' idea at TMcL works out in practice in the following ways:

1 Each local partnership remains just that—a local partnership, with a distinct legal and financial identity.
2 The cross-links between the constituent parts of the federation are provided by cross-partnerships, and by relatively minor direct financial arrangements.
3 Co-ordination of standards and policies is attained by a network of joint committees.

In England, the cross-partnership system means that the senior partner in each regional firm is also a partner in the London office; and two or more London partners are partners in the regional firm. Within Scotland the system is a little less 'reciprocal' in that the Glasgow office provides partners in the regional firms, but not at present vice versa. The system generates a high degree of awareness of what other parts of the federation are up to, and makes it most unlikely that any one office would embark on any substantial course of action which others disapproved of, while leaving a lot of initiative and authority in local hands.

Financially, in England and Scotland the London and Glasgow offices respectively take a small share stake in each regional firm, and there are of course agreements covering such matters as the use of the TMcL name. But the main financial question concerns profits. At one time treatment of the various parts of TMcL varied. London for example retained a big share in the profits of the Manchester and

Birmingham offices, which it had after all set up back in the 1920s; but in Newcastle and Bristol it had a share in the profits only over a certain base line. With the coming of a national rather than a London view of the organization, this difference clearly would not do, and a unified financial structure was adopted, which in effect meant that more rather than less money was left in local hands. London's share of profits was fixed at a nominal percentage for each regional firm, which equalled its low percentage of the capital. The main financial link between the various parts of TMcL is therefore the agreed sharing of certain expenses on the basis of either turnover or numbers of staff, those expenses being national expenses incurred by the activities of the various national committees, and international expenses incurred in developing the international organization of McLintock Main Lafrentz. Certain specialist services, like computer auditing, tend also to be based on London and Edinburgh and other offices which use them pay for doing so (as London pays if it uses a service provided by someone else).

Not surprisingly, the process of negotiating the various mergers in England and Scotland that went to make up the present-day firm was often a protracted and delicate one, requiring patience, diplomacy and long effort by the partners who carried out the negotiations. As one put it: 'Any one of them could have shown you the door.'

But that was the price for wooing firms which were well-established in their own right, with their own long histories, and which were worth having; and in the wooing of them, the fact that McLintocks could offer this loose federal structure—perhaps confederation might be a better word—was undoubtedly its unique selling point, to use a salesman's jargon, which more than offset the inevitable disappearance of the original name of the local firm in favour of the TMcL masthead. In Scotland the problems of courtship lead to a peculiarly Scottish system of trial engagements, in which, with the exception of the Edinburgh merger, each local office kept its separate name and identity for two to three years, but with a TMcL nameplate added to its door, before the local name disappeared in favour of Thomson McLintock & Co, and full confederal status was achieved.

So we have a situation in which there is no head office as such, no single unified partnership, no pooling of profits, and no one man to tell the others what to do. Conversely, there is a network of working arrangements, described in detail in another chapter, which bind the whole thing together and which are deliberately designed not only to preserve local autonomy but also to bring representatives of all the regional firms into the mainstream of decision-making and deliberation for the firm as a whole. This, then, was the philosophy with which Thomson McLintock & Co expanded and completed its coverage of England and Scotland, evolved an organizational structure to enable the various parts to move in unison, and which it applied simultaneously and consciously to the building up of McLintock Main Lafrentz internationally.

Chapter Eight

COMPLETING THE COVERAGE: ENGLAND AND WALES

BOTH THE Manchester and the Birmingham offices of TMcL date back to the 1920s—Birmingham in fact to 1921, when Sir William McLintock acquired the Birmingham practice of Charles Baker & Co, a small firm with a staff of six with one partner (HHH Walshe) although with a small list of quite important clients. But they remained the sole outposts of the empire (apart from the brief excursion to Paris) right through the inter-war period, the war years, and for some years after the war, although it is fair to add that the Manchester office did itself have its own offshoot in Sheffield as early as 1934; the Sheffield branch was to be the cause of a minor but interesting argument within TMcL during its later phase of expansion.

The first real sign of the new expansionist mood of McLintocks came in 1963, when the Birmingham office merged with the local firm of Aston Wilde. Prior to 1939, progress in Birmingham had been, by contemporary standards, unspectacular. The staff of six in 1921 rose to twenty-one by 1939, with two partners. But here again there was an illustration of how McLintock men have always played an important role in the world outside accountancy. In 1937 the then senior partner, RE Herington, was appointed to the position of secretary of what was known as the Aero Engine Committee which supervised the running of the shadow factories built at that time as part of a secret re-armaments programme in readiness for the war.

By way of a sequel, this particular appointment led to HM Pritchard of Birmingham serving on what was known as the Coventry Reconstruction Co-ordinating Committee which was set up on the instructions of the then Minister of Aircraft Production—Lord Beaverbrook—to get Coventry going again following the blitz on the city in 1940. Then, for some strange reason, he found himself in the company of representatives of the three armed services helping to establish priorities for the restitution of the public utility services—gas, water, electricity and telephones—to all the factories put out of action by the air raid.

As the war went on, nearly all the male staff left to join the services. But the continuing involvement of the office with the work of the Aero Engine Committee caused HM Pritchard and AA Davies to be exempt from military service, so that at a very early age they became key personnel in the firm, with Pritchard running the audit and general side of the office and Davies in charge of taxation work. This prepared them to play their part in the developments which followed the end of the war. These centred mainly round the Standard Motor Company, which set out on a policy of expansion which lasted for several years. During this time there was an almost ceaseless programme of special work coming into the office, including acquisitions of substantial companies who were suppliers to Standard of items such as castings, body work and sub-assemblies. The highlight of this special work was, however, the splitting up in 1959 of the Standard Motor Company into separate car and tractor companies to permit the sale of the tractor interests to Massey-Harris, a major task in which Pritchard and Davies played a leading part. It was undoubtedly the experience of those years which caused Birmingham to break away from its original concept of a small office servicing the local needs of London, and as a result Birmingham emerged as a firm of standing in its own right.

These developments were not free of problems; the firm had grown to a size when one partner was insufficient.

Pritchard, however, as an incorporated accountant, was not eligible, but with the encouragement of the London partners he served a second term of articles at a somewhat advanced age and passed the four examinations of the Scottish Institute. Promotion to partnership followed for Davies and Pritchard at the end of 1948. This increase in capacity at a time of growing complexity in accountancy and taxation affairs led to all the work then carried out on the local basis for London being transferred entirely to the Birmingham firm.

As a result, with a steady flow of new work also coming in, the office continued to grow steadily. It took a major leap forward, however, with the merger with Aston Wilde. The combined staff at the date of the merger was about fifty but in recent years the rate of growth has accelerated considerably and the staff is now over 100. The firm of Aston Wilde & Co must have been one of the earliest firms in Birmingham, practising originally as Smedley & Sargent, then as WS Aston & Earle and as Aston Wilde & Co from 1927. The date of formation of the original firm of Smedley & Sargent is not known but there is still in existence a time book of an articled clerk dating from 1879; that clerk later became famous as Sir John Ellerman of the shipping line.

The merger with Aston Wilde brought in a substantial amount of business, including two major clients with interests throughout the United Kingdom whose business was not all handled by Aston Wilde because it lacked the necessary coverage. All this potential business has since come into the firm, and in recent years Birmingham has been referring work to other offices.

RE Herington had retired in 1961, and although the merger with Aston Wilde increased the number of active partners to four they were clearly inadequate to deal with the rapid growth in the firm which followed the merger. This problem was overcome in two ways, both of which are of interest. First of all John Constantine, who had served his apprenticeship with the firm and was at the time secretary to the Standard Motor Company, was persuaded to rejoin the firm as a partner in 1964. Secondly, consideration was being given at this time to a closer working relationship between Birmingham and Leicester and RE Gordon, who had been established by London as a partner in Leicester, also became a partner in the Birmingham firm in 1968.

It is also of interest to note that, except for RE Gordon, Birmingham has been partnered throughout by local men. In contrast Manchester until recently has been partnered entirely by people sent up by London, and this probably explains why Birmingham has for a long time been established as an independent practice, not so dependent on referrals from London. Nevertheless, much of the growth in the last few years has been due to the substantial amount of work sent to Birmingham from both London and Glasgow.

For TMcL nationally, a big burst of merger activity followed in 1966, a date which is also interesting because it was the time at which the international organization was being set up, and shows how development of the two sides, national and international, clearly inter-related in the thinking and planning of the firm as a whole. The two substantial mergers of 1966 took the process of giving TMcL proper national coverage in England several steps further. These were the merger of the TMcL Newcastle office with the local firm of Squance and Co, and the merger into the Manchester office of the Leeds firm of Sir Charles H Wilson and Co.

The Newcastle office had been opened some years before, when TMcL gained the audit of the Essoldo cinema group, whose headquarters were in Newcastle. At about the same time the firm also gained the audit of a large shipbuilding concern in the area, and through this activity got to know and like Squance, thus leading to the merger; not the least recommendation of Squance and Co was that it is also 100 years old in 1977. The original Mr TC Squance was in fact in practice well before 1877, because there are River Wear commissioners and water company accounts certified by him in the 1850s—showing, incidentally, how TMcL has often taken over firms with roots going back further than its own. But the firm of TC Squance and Sons was formed in 1877 when the first son was taken into partnership.

The family had a strong Wesleyan religious background, but also a strong background of the sea; TC Squance's father was a clergyman who, in 1813, sailed with the pioneer Wesleyan mission to India, and his wife's father was a Sunderland shipowner. Squance himself was a Wesleyan like his sons after him, had a remarkable memory, a remarkable library and the habit of walking to and from work reciting to himself whole passages of scripture, hymns, or extracts from great authors. Several historical accounts of the firm contain the following story, without saying which of the Squances, with their knowledge of the sea, originated it:

'The Institute of Chartered Accountants started in 1880 and the original partners of TC Squance and Sons became chartered accountants without the formality of passing examinations. The Arms of the Institute in 1881 are described as:

' "Argent on a Mount in Base in front of a Rudder in bend sinister a Female figure proper representing 'Economy' habited Gules mantled Azure about the temples a Wreath of Olive in the dexter hand a Rod and in the sinister a pair of Compasses."

'The fact that the lady has a rudder presumably symbolizes the responsibility of chartered accountants in leading their clients along the straight and narrow path wherein virtue lies. One glance, however, at the coat of arms would indicate to any member of the sea staff that as the lady has her helm set hard aport she must be describing small circles to starboard! Most accountants know that feeling only too well.'

In 1948 the old established firm of John Parker and Sons was taken over by Squance and then in 1962 another old established firm, Rawlings and Wilkinson, was taken over, and the name altered to Squance and Co. It is interesting to note that all three constituent firms were operating before the English Institute was set up in 1880, and also shows how the final merger with TMcL was, in Newcastle as elsewhere, just the culmination of a long process of consolidation of the accountancy profession in the area.

The year 1966 also saw the beginning of a new era in the Manchester office, first with a merger and then with new people at the helm. The story of Manchester is worth telling in some detail, both for its intrinsic interest, and because it illustrates the ups and downs that have characterized out-of-London offices in England.

In 1919, Sir William McLintock summoned the following to meet him in a large room in the Midland Hotel, Manchester; TC Guthrie and an assistant from London; Wm Anderson and an assistant from Glasgow; Harold Bland, who had been engaged as the first qualified assistant in Manchester. The object of the gathering was the work on the amalgamation of British Dyes Ltd, Huddersfield, and Levinstein Ltd, Manchester, to form the beginning of what is now the Dyestuffs Division of ICI. Thus was born the Manchester business, with a staff of three—Bland, an office boy (Herbert Mills, for many years with the firm and later a senior executive in Yorkshire of the National Coal Board) and a typist.

At first, the work consisted mainly of audits on London jobs with branches or factories in Lancashire and the north of England. In the meantime, largely influenced by the growing taxation work in London for the colliery industry, a connection with the Lancashire coal owners was being established. In the next ten years the amalgamations forming Manchester Collieries Ltd, Hargreaves Collieries Ltd, and The Wigan Coal Corporation Ltd, were carried through in the London office. There was also the amalgamation of the Lancashire steel trade, then at a low ebb, to form the Lancashire Steel Corporation Ltd, with financial aid from the Bank of England. The firm was appointed auditors of these new companies and, to save time and expense, the audits were carried out mainly by staff resident in Manchester but supervised by the London office where the accounts were ultimately signed. The same arrangement applied to the audits of what are now divisions and subsidiaries of ICI in the north of England.

By 1928 the Manchester office had expanded to the point at which a resident partner was required and Robert Paterson was sent from London to take charge, and became the first Manchester partner in 1930. By that date the foundations of a good business had been laid, although very much controlled and supervised by the London office. Robert Paterson was offered and accepted the secretaryship of the Lancashire Steel Corporation in 1933. For some years previously, Sir William had stated from time to time that he intended to send TC Guthrie to Manchester as a second partner, but pressure of work in London had prevented the move. When Paterson suddenly decided to leave the firm, Guthrie was recalled from holiday and instructed to take over immediately.

Thus began his twenty-five years in charge of the Manchester office. Since 1930, Guthrie had been one of the assistants to Sir William on the work in connection with the financial collapse of the Kylsant Shipping Group, his duties being largely concerned with the companies with headquarters in Liverpool. As a result of the Royal Mail and Elder Dempster schemes of arrangement and the general clean-up of the financial chaos of the group, TMcL was, as we have seen, appointed auditors of several of the companies. After Guthrie's arrival in Manchester, the audits of the Liverpool shipping companies, Elder Dempster Lines and Moss Hutchison Line, were transferred from London to Manchester and, at a much later date, the audit of the Pacific Steam Navigation Company, whose head office was in Liverpool, was also transferred, it being a subsidiary of Royal Mail Lines, whose accounts were done by the London office.

After 1933 the control and supervision by the London office was almost wholly relaxed and for many years the Manchester office, as regards work for clients, functioned independently of London, except for joint work such as ICI.

About the time that TMcL opened an office in Manchester, several of the large London accountancy firms also opened offices in Manchester; the old-established Manchester accountants regarded the newcomers as interlopers and there were undoubtedly hard feelings about this for a number of years. Later, this resentment seems to have disappeared.

But Manchester then suffered very heavily from the great contraction of the cotton textile trade. This affected hundreds of businesses in the various sections of this once vast trade and there were heavy capital losses. There was expansion in engineering and aircraft, but these developing industries were not locally owned and were mainly controlled by large companies with headquarters in London.

Many old-established accountancy firms in the Manchester area lost more than half their practice. These depressed conditions and capital losses made it difficult to expand an accountancy practice of the TMcL type as compared with a more prosperous area. The Manchester office also suffered a severe setback when the colliery industry was nationalized at the end of 1946. The firm were accountants to the Lancashire coal owners. One quarter of the total fees came from work for this industry on audits, taxation, wages ascertainments and general work such as odd investigations and prospectuses. This work, mainly of an annual recurring nature, disappeared overnight. There was a very substantial loss of annual fees, although for a number of years after 1946 this was to some extent off-set by nationalization and colliery valuation work and liquidations of the old colliery companies.

The loss of the colliery connection was in time largely made good by new business from other quarters, and TMcL became auditors to the National Coal Board which replaced the old colliery companies. More recently, Manchester has been reinvigorated with the arrival of three new partners from London in the few years up to 1970, all determined to show what they could do in terms of generating local business; by a fortunate coincidence, TMcL at about this time gained the audit of the Co-operative Wholesale Society,

Mr James T Dowling

Mr Thomas Lister

based largely in the Manchester area. It was this situation that caused the argument about Sheffield. For, true to pattern, TMcL had been looking for a local Sheffield firm to assimilate with its Sheffield office, and had indeed found one and reached an advanced stage of negotiation, when the Manchester partners pointed out that a big TMcL firm in Sheffield would cramp their efforts to give Manchester a substantial practice of its own. This objection carried the day, and Sheffield remained unmerged; but the incident showed as clearly as any other the inter-active, non-authoritarian way in which the firm arrives at its decisions.

The Leeds firm of Sir Charles H Wilson and Co which amalgamated with Manchester in 1966 was founded only months before his death in 1930 by Sir Charles Wilson, as remarkable a man in his own sphere as Sir William was in his.

Born at Brandsby, Easingwold, Yorkshire, in 1859, Charles Henry Wilson began his career as a railway clerk, but soon after going to Leeds went into business as an accountant and later became a Fellow of the Society of Incorporated Accountants and Auditors, of which he was president during the years 1901–04. In 1890 he became a Leeds councillor and began a career in which he dominated the local political scene for almost forty years.

His peak was undoubtedly 1923, when he was created a knight in recognition of his services to local politics and following his spell as Lord Mayor of Leeds; was made a Freeman of Leeds; received the honorary degree of LLD of Leeds University; and became Conservative MP for Central Leeds. He served as Member of Parliament for this Leeds constituency until his death. He was often referred to as 'Cheeky Charlie' by his political opponents. There was something affectionate in the disrespect, and probably meant no more than that he cut no corners in speaking. He weighed nineteen stone and his style of battle was in the heavyweight class; opponents were apt to get clouted hard. No one, though, got more hard clouts than Charles Wilson himself, and he took them like the big man he was, as the expected price of political warfare.

Two of Charles Wilson's major contributions to Leeds were his advocacy of boundary extension and the part he played in securing for Leeds, for £35,000, the mansion and park of Temple Newsam. 'I am Leeds' was a famous phrase he uttered in 1921 at a boundary extension inquiry in Leeds. The phrase was taken out of its context to suggest he was self-important; in fact, he was merely stating that he was the Leeds representative there. He died in 1930, at the age of 71.

After the Squance and Wilson mergers it became clear that there was one major area of England in which McLintocks was still seriously under-represented and that was the south-west, meaning in effect Bristol. This was despite a long and interesting association with this area dating back to before the second world war. As early as 1935, the Bristol Aeroplane Company had become a client of TMcL, and indeed TMcL helped the company to go public in that year. Later, two McLintock managers joined the staff of the Bristol Aero Company, and one of them rose to become finance director of the British Aircraft Corporation, into which parts of the Bristol company were merged. Because of this work, there was a TMcL office actually inside the Bristol Areoplane works, and apart from that there was also a small Cardiff office to work on Coal Board matters.

However, as the Bristol Aeroplane work gradually began to disappear as the company itself began to disappear through a complex series of mergers of its constituent parts into BAC and into Rolls-Royce, it was obvious that a fresh look was needed at this geographical area. McLintocks turned to Grace Darbyshire and Todd, and a merger followed in 1969. Without disrespect to any of the other constituent parts of TMcL it is fair to say that the Bristol firm was not then just the largest (a staff of 140 and 11 partners currently) but also the most distinctive addition to the McLintock federation, with an assertive commercially-minded approach that could not fail to have a big impact on the firm as a whole.

The Bristol practice is also the second oldest constituent (by one year) of the present day Thomson McLintock & Co, tracing its history back to 1818, when John Moxham, a Quaker, set up in business in Bristol. Nearly forty years later, in 1857, his practice was absorbed by the recently established Grace family, also strongly Quaker; for three generations the Graces provided all the partners in the firm until in 1919 and 1920 the admission of two non-family partners caused the name to be changed to Grace Darbyshire and Todd. Up to 1946 all partners of the firm except one were Quakers.

In 1957 the firm celebrated its centenary; but it is since its centenary that the firm's period of rapid change set in. For in 1962 the firm formed two unit trusts under the title of the Tyndall Funds to undertake for its clients the management of the considerable investment portfolios which had, for many years, been under the control of the firm. This venture was started in a very modest way but its rapid development caused the partnership, in the autumn of 1965, to separate its ownership and activities from those of the firm. A new company, Tyndall Ltd, was set up to own and run the Tyndall Funds, and although the partners and their families owned its share capital, it was conducted as a quite separate entity under Ernest Harbottle as executive chairman; later it acquired the business of Jordan and Sons, company registration and law agents, founded in 1863.

Behind this bare set of facts lies a long tradition of commercial operation. The early Graces had listed among their activities 'purchases and sales of stock and shares', and 'executors and trustees'. By the 1950s the firm found that it had a considerable problem in supervising a large number of investment portfolios, and realized that the management of these portfolios would be a lot simpler if they were consolidated into one or two large funds; hence the Tyndall Income and Tyndall Capital Funds were formed (Tyndall is an old Bristol name). For two years the funds were carried on without publicity; then in 1964 it was decided to advertise the funds, and the response was far greater than the partners anticipated. This, plus the setting up of several other funds between 1965 and 1969 to cope with client problems arising out of the 1965 Finance Act and the Capital Gains Tax it introduced, were the immediate reasons for 'hiving off' the Tyndall Funds into a separate company, since it threatened to unbalance the whole operation; it is also true that the 'hiving off' would have been essential anyway because of the changing climate of opinion about professional involvement in investment work. But conversely, the 'hiving off' of Tyndall clarified the business of Grace Darbyshire as accountants, and its merger, first with the local firm of CJ Ryland and Co in 1967, and with TMcL in 1969, must be seen in this light.

Rylands was itself an old established Bristol firm, which had ironically once been housed in the same building as the Grace practice. CJ Ryland himself died in 1909, and later there was to be seen hanging on the office wall a framed epitaph to him, written with humour and a hint of affection by one of the staff. It read:

Hic jacet CJ RYLAND, man precise
In whom precision was a vice
Closed his account, and drawn his latest breath,
His presence lingers, e'en in Death
But if, in common with all mortals,
He'd find himself at Heaven's portals,
And sneaking past the watchful sentry
Should shuffle through by double entry
He'd use his wiles—who could resist 'em,
Teaching angels book-keeping, his own pet system.

Auditing now seems an altogether more serious business, and for the Bristol firm the merger with TMcL brought a substantial expansion of audit practice in the south-west of England, the transfer to its supervision of the McLintock office in Cardiff (still small) and the opening in 1974 of an Exeter branch office, due to growth of work there and improved road links from Bristol to Exeter. What the Bristol firm brought to Thomson McLintock & Co was a commercial instinct and attitude, a determination not to repeat the type of mistakes that had marred its previous attempt to link with another large firm, and an equal determination to play its part in the affairs of TMcL nation-wide. This last has found its expression in, for example, one Bristol partner (Donald Ironside) being a leading architect of the firm's present organization structure and also one of the three-man steering committee that guides the firm. In short, Bristol is the best (but not the only) example of a local firm that was (and remains) very conscious of being 'their own men' not likely to submerge their identity into some impersonal monolith.

McLintocks was first represented in Belfast during 1970. The firm (interestingly, through an MML introduction) brought into association a small Belfast practice which had been set up by Nigel May in 1965 under the name May & Co. The practice was still very small, but the introduction of TMcL work brought further expansion so that staff numbers now approach thirty. During its short history, the practice has survived a 200 lb bomb outside the front door, and the enthusiasm and loyalty of the staff throughout the Northern Ireland troubles demonstrate an atmosphere in which Catholic and Protestant have always worked side by side. The principal clients in Northern Ireland include a number of substantial subsidiaries of the Courtaulds Group, British Enkalon, a daily newspaper, and, through London, the Northern Bank.

Life has been rather less hazardous at the latest addition to the McLintock federation. Thomson McLintock Leicester was created by the merger in January 1974 of Baker Bros Halford & Co and the small office established by Thomson McLintock London in the fifties to service its clients in the Leicester area. Baker Bros Halford consisted of the original firm of that name and three other Leicester practices which had joined it at various times since 1965, once again illustrating the cumulative nature of merger activity in a particular locality.

The practice was established by Edward Roberts in about 1868. Roberts, like many of his contemporaries, was engaged solely in liquidation work until the impetus came to act as auditor to companies. One of the earliest records extant is a copy of the balance sheet of the Ibstock Colliery Company certified by Edwards Roberts in 1877. Ibstock, now Ibstock Johnsen Limited, is still a client of the firm. In 1872 Roberts was joined by JH Baker and in 1880 by AJ Halford, and when JH Baker's brother, Feldon, with a Northampton practice, joined the firm it became Baker Bros & Halford. In 1922 Feldon Baker left the partnership, taking the Northampton practice with him. This practice was to become the Baker side of Thornton Baker & Co. In 1965 the firm of ER Carr & Co joined with Baker Bros & Halford, and in 1967 E Carpendale Corton, founded in 1931, also joined. Hopps and Bankart, which had been formed in about 1880, then joined Baker Bros in 1968. TMcL's small Leicester office had been a classic instance of the basic problem that a small office, probably with only one partner, is simply not in a position to expand and 'go for growth'. The 1974 Leicester merger therefore completed the geographical coverage of England as it is now.

But 1975 brought one further change in the structure of the English operation. The firm had begun to develop a management services practice in London in 1959. This was done in conjunction with two other firms of Scottish chartered accountants; Brown, Fleming & Murray and Mann Judd & Co. The three firms together formed the consultant practice of McLintock Mann & Murray, a name which was later changed to McLintock Mann & Whinney Murray when Brown, Fleming & Murray became Whinney Murray & Co. This was a multi-discipline firm and for many years the managing partner was not an accountant but an engineer.

In 1964 the firm acquired a small IBM/1440 which was used to provide services for all three firms, including the time records for McLintocks. It is believed that this was the first computer operated in the UK by an accounting firm, and with the very substantial development costs of computer systems, all three firms have at times regretted that they were pioneers in this field.

Until 1972/73 the turnover of MM & WM, including the turnover of the computer bureau (by then equipped with an IBM/360), increased steadily. Much of the consultancy work was done for clients who were not clients of the three main firms, although the limitations on advertising due to being associated with professional accounting firms meant that outside work was not so easy to obtain. So when a recession developed in the United Kingdom and excess capacity appeared among consultancy firms, the work load began to fall off. In the autumn of 1975 Whinney Murray and McLintocks therefore decided that the consultancy firm should be 'slimmed down' (Mann Judd had already left the consortium some months earlier). This decision was taken partly for economic reasons, and partly because of the growing realization of the disadvantages of a joint operation between two firms who were otherwise competitors, both in the United Kingdom and internationally. Both firms therefore determined to build up their own management services practices, but with the registration and computer bureau side of the joint firm continuing for the time being. A number of consultants from MM & WM joined the staff of McLintocks, and a separate management services department was formed. The whole operation was put under the control of Nigel May in London, it having been agreed that management services in England should be developed as one unit based in London, but providing the service for all the English offices.

The process of completing the coverage in England and Wales was therefore a rather English blend of chance and planning, a mixture of *ad hoc* answers to specific local problems and situations, and deliberate thought-out policy. In Scotland, events were much more the result of a conscious decision to 'cover the waterfront' in response to a well-defined challenge from TMcL's competitors.

Chapter Nine

COMPLETING THE COVERAGE: SCOTLAND

A QUICK LOOK at the growth tree of Thomson McLintock & Co might suggest that the expansion of the firm to cover the whole of Scotland was, with the exception of Aberdeen, largely accomplished in one year, 1975. There is some truth in this, for 1975 was indeed a very active year, involving Edinburgh, Dundee and Inverness, and in a negative sense East Kilbride, where a short-lived office opened in 1973 on an experimental basis at the invitation of the local development corporation was shut in October of 1975 because the town simply did not generate business on the right scale.

But the seeds of recent developments in Scotland go back twenty years or more, and were first planted by that greatest single figure in the Scottish firm's post-war history, James Dowling. During the second world war, much of McLintocks' business in Scotland had not been commercial work at all, but concerned with industries like bread, milk and coal which came under government regulation as part of the war effort. As a result McLintocks' reputation for commercial work had to be virtually re-established after the war ended, as government regulation of these industries (or in the case of coal, nationalization) brought that type of work to a close. It was Dowling who set about the job.

Thanks to his own personal reputation as an accountant, and because he was in effect senior partner in Glasgow from about 1955 onwards, due to John Duncan's growing ill-health, he began to travel a great deal around Scotland, getting the firm known again and laying the foundation for future expansion. It was an era during which a lot of Scottish quoted companies were absorbed by larger and usually non-Scottish groups, and though this meant in the long run loss of work to Scottish accountants, in the short run it meant that people who were selling their businesses turned to him for professional advice and services. He also did a great deal of work in amalgamation of investment trusts. Thanks to his efforts, McLintocks not only regained a solid commercial reputation, but also confirmed its position as probably the largest single accountancy firm in Scotland at that time.

Both of these assets were to prove invaluable later, when in the mid-1960s the big London-based and international accountancy firms began to expand into Scotland, which had hitherto been the preserve of the Scots. Following the trend of international business, the big firms began to absorb the Scottish accountants one by one, city by city, and the series of moves by McLintocks from 1965 onwards to gain representation in all major centres in Scotland was essentially a reaction, call it defensive or offensive as you will, to this invasion by 'outsiders'. Clearly, McLintocks would have lost or at least failed to gain a great deal of business if it had not met the challenge, although the firm itself received no formal proposals for a merger.

It is therefore to the credit of Dowling that McLintocks was by the mid-1960s not only too large a fish for other firms to swallow, especially with its London connection, but was also soundly enough based in Scotland to become one of the very few substantial native firms not to 'go under' but on the contrary to meet the challengers at their own game. We have already seen how Dowling negotiated the reunion with the London office in 1959. This was the first tangible sign of the new status and spirit of the Scottish firm, and while a natural answer to business developments at the time, it was also another asset in meeting the challenge of the 1960s.

But there were other innovations in 1959 also. A small

management accounting department was set up, which was to grow into something bigger. There was of course nothing new in accountants undertaking management accounting. But after the war many businesses required a thorough rethinking of their system of accounting and at that time it began to be the fashion to call this work by a specific name, whereas previously consultancy of this type would have been regarded as giving rise, perhaps, to special fees. Basically, the problem with consultancy was and is that it requires knowledge of industry as well as of accounting, and in any one firm there would not necessarily be enough on-going work for a highly paid member of staff. So on the basis of the 1959 beginnings, a separate joint firm of McLintock, Moores and Murray was established in 1962 at 156 St Vincent Street, Glasgow. The initial partners in this new venture were Thomson McLintock & Co; McClelland, Moores & Co; and Brown, Fleming & Murray, all of Glasgow. Later, other firms took an interest. Thomson McLintock and the other participants always stressed the fact that the work of the management consulting company was an extension of its traditional practice which, for practical considerations, could more effectively be carried on in conjunction with others.

Then about 1973 consultancy went out of fashion. In the words of a Glasgow partner, companies previously called in consultants and it was a credit to them, giving an up-to-date panache; then it suddenly became fashionable to throw out consultants. As a result the composite firm ceased to exist with the falling away of interest, and was replaced, so far as TMcL was concerned, by Thomson McLintock Associates Ltd which serves the whole Scottish practice.

The next event in Scotland was the opening of an office in Edinburgh in 1965; but there was already a long history behind this too. During the evolution of the Scottish practice up to and after the second world war the firm had become involved in a clientèle which stretched across the whole of Scotland. Client work in the north was wholly dealt with by staff travelling to clients' premises, and, frequently, by clients visiting the Glasgow office for consultation. This situation was bound to warrant a change in both the attitude of the firm and of its clients, and the first major step in regionalization took place as early as 1949 when Thomson McLintock & Co became auditors of the National Coal Board and were required to service the Scottish headquarters of the Board, in Edinburgh. The old-established firm of A & CM Davidson Smith, CA Edinburgh, with whom TMcL had already had a long and friendly association, were appointed agents to TMcL with the task of providing an audit service to the NCB in Edinburgh under the jurisdiction of the responsible partner in Glasgow. This association went on for fifteen years or so, until in 1965 the firm decided that its practice in the east of Scotland, including the audit of the NCB, was sufficiently substantial, and had been so for some years, that it was desirable to open its own office in Edinburgh. This was done at 25 St Andrew Square.

This first formal move outside Glasgow is, however, to be seen in conjunction with two other events. One was the amalgamation of the Edinburgh, Glasgow and Aberdeen societies of accountants to form The Institute of Chartered Accountants of Scotland in 1951. Before that there was an unwritten law that no chartered accountancy firm of Glasgow should have a place of work in Edinburgh!

The other was the merger of a large Edinburgh firm of accountants with another of the big international firms, Deloittes; the opening of the Edinburgh office was McLintocks' first move in the new game of survival.

While justified as a pilot operation, the Edinburgh office was not, however, a totally successful venture. Edinburgh was a difficult place to break into for an outsider, even (or, perhaps, particularly!) for one from Glasgow. So the paradox developed that almost all the established Edinburgh firms were one by one swallowed up by the big groups, while the branch office of a native Scots firm was struggling to keep its foothold. In the end, however, the struggle proved justified, for the Edinburgh firm which was one of the oldest and proudest in the city, and had long held out against absorption, had a change of heart and went in with the firm which most shared its outlook, Thomson McLintock & Co. The Edinburgh firm was Robertson & Maxtone Graham, and because there was an already established McLintock office in Edinburgh, the usual pattern of 'trial marriages' between McLintocks and a prospective partner was not followed, but a full and immediate merger was arranged. This meant that the Edinburgh firm's eleven general partners came in with the Glasgow firm's eighteen partners at the time, which not only showed the almost equal size of the two units, but made the combined unit one of the largest in British accountancy outside London. Edinburgh's two investment management partners hived themselves off elsewhere, by amicable arrangement.

Robertson & Maxtone Graham was, in fact, a much older firm than McLintocks, having been formed by the merging of the Edinburgh firm of A & J Robertson with Maxtone Graham & Sime in 1961 and with Wm Home Cook & Coy in 1972; one of the constituent parts of Wm Home Cook dated back to 1817, making it the oldest known root of the modern UK firm. Later, it was Mr AW Robertson of A & J Robertson who approached fourteen practising accountants in Edinburgh inviting them to join him in establishing a professional society. The outcome was the formation in 1854 of the Society of Accountants in Edinburgh, oldest of the constituent societies of the present Institute of Chartered Accountants of Scotland and the oldest organized accounting body in the world; Mr Robertson became the first secretary of the Edinburgh society.

Another interesting historical facet of the merger concerned Mr J Maxtone Graham who practised in Edinburgh, London and Montreal from the late 19th century to the 1920s. In addition to his name forming part of Robertson & Maxtone Graham it also featured in the name of Riddell Stead Graham & Hutchison, Chartered Accountants, Canada, who are now incorporated in Thorne Riddell & Co, Chartered Accountants, Canada, one of the participators, with Thomson McLintock & Co and others, in the international firm McLintock Main Lafrentz. The wheel, it could be said, had come full circle.

The McLintock move into Aberdeen came not long after the setting up of the Edinburgh office, in 1968, and took the form of a link with G & J McBain. In Aberdeen, as was to happen also in Dundee and Inverness, the more typically McLintock procedure was followed, with a period of several years of 'trial marriage', or 'arranged engagement' as others have preferred to call it, before a more substantial commitment was entered into. In the case of G & J McBain, the trial period was three years, the final merger taking place in 1971.

Founded in 1888, G & J McBain had had a long association with Thomson McLintock and had consulted them in an advisory capacity on many occasions since the first world war. The two firms were also associated as joint auditors of G & G Kynoch Ltd since 1954 and had further associations through The Glenlivet Distillers Ltd.

Some clients have been with the Aberdeen firm virtually since its inception. The earliest list available is for 1902 and discloses the following clients who are still with the firm:

Aberdeen Savings Bank
Aberdeen Soup Kitchen
Aberdeen University Press
Forgue Savings Bank
Granite Supply Association
Hugh Imlay & Co
Mitchell & Muil

Throughout its history the firm's clientèle has included most of the traditional industries of the north-east of Scotland —fishing, granite, engineering, agriculture, papermaking, textiles, shipping, shipbuilding and whisky distilling. There has also been a good representation of the wholesale and retail establishments in and around the city as well as a number of professional clients, investment trusts and insurance companies. The development of the North Sea oil industry in the last few years has brought new and significant clients, some with international connections.

It will be seen that almost all the initiatives so far detailed took place while James Dowling was in charge of the Glasgow firm. But Dowling retired in 1969, and a short pause ensued in the progress of the firm. The successor to Dowling was John Waldie, who had joined the firm in 1931, left it in 1936 for five years in commerce, and after the war became well known for his work on the pre-nationalization problems of the coal industry. He was a distinguished accountant, but rather like JC Burleigh and Sir John Morison at an earlier time in the London office, was not inclined to be adventurous. As a result, the process of expansion halted for several years, and the next move was not seen until 1973, with the 'big blitz' on the situation in 1975. Waldie retired in 1974, after an honourable tenure of office, and his place was taken by two joint senior partners, John Kirkpatrick and Bill Morrison, the former a nephew of Thomas Lister, the latter yet another 'distinction' man, and both of them younger men who energetically set about completion of McLintock's coverage of Scotland, spurred on by the knowledge that by 1975 there were few independent firms left that were suitable for merger and so time was very short. The policy was to go for units of forty to fifty people, with partners who could continue local control, and McLintocks often got the last, if the best, fruit on the local tree.

The Dundee firm with whom McLintocks followed its normal practice of 'arranged engagement' in 1973, followed by marriage in 1975, was Moody Stuart & Robertson. Dundee is, of course, a great centre for investment trusts, dating back to the overseas business of the city's 'jute kings', and the business of the Dundee firm reflected this. James Robertson, a co-founder of the firm in 1875, was a contemporary of the founders and later of the managers of the companies which ran these investment trusts (directed mainly at investment in the USA and Canada), and was auditor of:

Matador Land & Cattle Co
The Alliance Trust Co
The Western & Hawaiian Investment Co (later the Second Alliance Trust Co)
Northern American Trust Co
First Scottish American Trust Co
Second Scottish American Trust Co
Third Scottish American Trust Co

The audits of these companies continue with the firm with the exception of the Matador Land & Cattle Co which was taken over by North American interests in 1951.

Robertson's strong personality at times brought him into conflict with boards of directors. At the annual meeting of the Matador Land and Cattle Co in 1907 Robertson in a somewhat lengthy speech criticized the costs of management, the American manager's travelling expenses and his association with the American Stock Growers Association. Before sitting down he stated that he was about to travel on business and pleasure in Mexico, the United States and Canada and that he would visit two of the company's ranches and would report thereon 'without cost to the company'.

The manager made a spirited reply. Robertson did visit the ranches and having been received with every courtesy, reported by mail, withdrawing his criticisms of the manager. He remained auditor until 1930 and never again spoke critically of management expenses at a shareholders' meeting of that company.

Despite such interludes, investment trust work, as auditors or secretaries, has been a mainstay of the Dundee business all this century.

The year 1975 also saw the full merger with the Edinburgh firm, already narrated, and an 'arranged engagement' with

Sir William Slimmings

Mr John L Kirkpatrick

a firm in Inverness, Frame Kennedy & Forrest. Not only did the Inverness firm bring with it a string of branch offices in the northern parts of Scotland, so completing to the satisfaction of the new joint senior partners the McLintock coverage of Scotland, but it also brought its own highly individual history. It seems that the accountancy profession in Inverness largely developed from one firm, Robert F Cameron & Forrest, which later fragmented as its partners set up on their own. As the firm's own notes put it:

'A feature of the profession in the time before and after the second world war was the rivalry of the more senior members, particularly those who had founded their own firms. The rivalry and personality clashes built up over the years delayed the amalgamation process taking place in other parts of the country. It was not until 1970 that the first amalgamation took place in Inverness between two firms both of which had originally sprung from Robert F Cameron & Forrest.

'It was clear that the practice of John C Frame & Co and Wm H Kennedy & Co would marry extremely well providing a joint firm with strength both in the immediate Inverness area and in other areas, particularly the North West and the Spey Valley. This took place (after the respective retirals of Wm H Kennedy and JC Frame) on 1 April 1971.

'After the inevitable settling down period it became clear that a larger unit would have substantial advantages. The client location of Robert F Cameron & Forrest combined successfully with those of Frame Kennedy, giving additional strength to the Inverness and Spey Valley areas and a reasonable presence in the Western Isles. Hence the amalgamation between the firms on 1 April 1973.

'In the same year it was decided to increase the firm's coverage of the north of Scotland as there was considered to be a considerable potential for new work in this area and in Orkney. Accordingly a branch office was opened in Thurso in August 1973. In 1975 it was recognized that there would be considerable advantages in an association with a larger firm. The firm therefore formed an association with Thomson McLintock & Co.'

If anyone still doubts that McLintocks in Scotland, as in England, had by preference or necessity to merge with local firms that were highly idiosyncratic and individualistic in their own right, and therefore had to adopt a loose organizational framework capable of coping with them, then surely this frank account of life among the accountants of Inverness must finally dispel such doubts.

At all events, after the hectic year of 1975, it was fully hoped that a period of calm and consolidation would set in, with the primary objective achieved of becoming a pan-Scottish firm; and it was not long before the rewards of this began to show. As not only a substantial firm in Scotland but also one that is still essentially Scottish, McLintocks was almost bound to benefit from the trend towards greater Scottish political independence. For example, after the reorganization of local government structure in the UK, McLintocks for the first time ever in Scotland applied for local authority audit work, and were allocated the sub-region of Glasgow, one of the largest units in the Scottish local authority system; the Inverness office retained work previously held but now incorporated the Highland region. Similarly, North Sea oil generates new business, not so much (but leaving aside the later mentioned new British National Oil Corporation connection) from the oil companies themselves, which have their own international firms of auditors, but from associated activities based in Scotland itself. Remarkably enough, the Scottish firm is still, as it always has been, a net exporter of business to other parts of the McLintock and the McLintock Main Lafrentz federations, and is therefore not relying on referred work. With one senior partner, Bill Morrison, attending mainly (but by no means wholly, for he is chairman of TMcL's audit group, co-chairman of MML's accounting and auditing committee and also MML's liaison man with the Middle East!) to domestic matters on the Scottish scene with nearly fifty partners, and the other, John Kirkpatrick, directing his attention to the UK national and international firms, the Scottish end of Thomson McLintock can therefore fairly be said to have reasserted in the 1960s and 1970s the position of initiative within the wider McLintock federation that it lost as far back as the 1920s.

The Scottish and London offices of Thomson McLintock & Co have made a marked contribution to the affairs of The Institute of Chartered Accountants of Scotland. Apart from three presidents (with John Kirkpatrick presently in line to be the fourth) since the Institute amalgamation in 1951, and a number of presidents in the predecessor bodies, TMcL and its constituents have provided many members of council over the years together with almost continuous representation on major committees. In addition to John Kirkpatrick the offices presently provide three members of council and also the conveners of four main standing committees.

Chapter Ten

THE LONDON OFFICE: 1959 TO THE PRESENT

NOT SURPRISINGLY, the period since 1959 has been a hectic one for the London office. In chapter 8, we have seen how the reintegration of the London and Glasgow offices in 1959 became the prelude to a series of mergers designed to complete the firm's coverage of England. In chapters 13 and 14, we shall see how this period also saw the initiation and development of the international firm of McLintock Main Lafrentz. These themes, although important in the life of the London office, will not be dealt with here. But the period also saw the physical move to the London firm's present premises at Finsbury Pavement, the accession to senior partnership of, first, Gerald Bradley and then Sir William Slimmings, substantial growth in numbers of staff and partners, and the development of the modern business climate of ever more complex tax laws, increased legal liabilities for accountants and new accounting standards, and a mass of special investigation work.

Thomas Lister, co-pilot of the 1959 reintegration, remained in office as London senior partner until 1967. In February of that year, it was announced that he would retire in March. Later in February, he paid what was thought to be a routine visit to hospital, and underwent an operation. Sadly, he died only a few days later. On his death, it was the unanimous wish of the partners that Gerald Bradley should take over, even though he himself was now nearing retiring age.

Bradley, as narrated in chapter 3, had been the first indentured apprentice in the London office, and it was in November 1967 that a private dinner party was held in London for partners and wives to celebrate Bradley's fifty years of continuous service. Bradley therefore had seen the London office grow from practically nothing to the substantial business that it then was. He had become a partner in 1946, and by making him senior partner his colleagues demonstrated the high regard they had both for the man and for the contribution he had made towards building up the London office. Bradley's guidance also helped a great deal towards the establishment of McLintock Main Lafrentz, and he was joint chairman of the second general conference of MML, held in Cambridge in September 1967.

Apart from his home and family, the firm was virtually Bradley's only interest, and throughout his career he drove himself hard—sometimes too hard for a none too robust constitution—to further its progress. Like his contemporary and great friend, James Dowling in Glasgow, he was a natural confidant both to his clients and his partners, a man to whom they turned when they needed sound advice, quietly and sympathetically given.

It was therefore another sad event when Bradley also proved unable to complete his full term of office as senior partner. In September 1968 he fell ill during a visit to an MML conference in America. He was away from work for several weeks, and was then advised by his doctor to discontinue full time work; he resigned at the end of September. It had been hoped that Bradley would be able to continue as senior partner until his expected (and actual) successor, Sir William Slimmings, had completed his term as vice-president and then president of the Scottish Institute, which was then in the thick of discussions and meetings about the integration of the various accountancy bodies in the United Kingdom. But it was not to be, and Sir William had to take over when he was already heavily committed elsewhere.

After his education at Dunfermline High School Sir William was in 1929 apprenticed to AC Philp & Co, Chartered Accountants, of that town. He passed his final CA examination in 1934 with distinction and was awarded the Sir John Mann prize. He had won a number of class medals on the road to qualifying; some of these were gained at Heriot-Watt College whose successor body, Heriot-Watt University, conferred upon him the Honorary Degree of Doctor of Letters in 1970. He joined TMcL in London in 1935 becoming a partner in 1946.

Sir William's term as senior partner spans the period 1968 to the present, and it is fair to say that in that time, and indeed before it, he has sustained the tradition of public service and prestige appointments that was such a feature of the great figure of the firm's past. Sir William, who had been appointed CBE in 1960, was knighted in 1966 for his work over nine years as chairman of the Board of Trade Advisory Committee dealing with grants to development areas. His presidency of the Scottish Institute at a critical period has just been mentioned; he was only the second Scottish accountant practising outside Scotland to hold that office, the first having been that other TMcL man, Thomas Lister.

Many people regard it as unfortunate that the work on integration of the accountancy profession that occupied so much of Sir William's time (and of many other people's time) at this juncture, should in the end have proved abortive.

Sir William's public career had begun as early as 1947, when he joined the Committee of Inquiry on the Cost of Housebuilding; in 1952 came the Committee on Tax-paid Stocks, and in 1955 the Committee on Cheque Endorsement. In 1963 he joined the Performing Right Tribunal. Since his period at the Scottish Institute there have come appointments to the Scottish Tourist Board; as chairman of the Review Board for government contracts; as adviser to several banks in relation to the affairs of Rolls-Royce, and subsequently as joint liquidator of Rolls-Royce Ltd; to a three-man committee to look into the purchasing arrangements of the National Coal Board; as one of the official inspectors to look into the affairs of Lonrho, the multi-national trading company which had seen a spectacular board-room row; as a member of the Review Body on Doctors' and Dentists' Remuneration; as a member of the Accounting Standards Committee and, most important of all, in 1976, as its chairman.

In the meantime had come the upheaval of moving from the premises in King William Street, where the firm had been since 1949, to the new and present building. Early in 1970 the threat, which had been in the offing for some time due to the rebuilding of London Bridge, materialized in the form of a letter stating that a compulsory purchase order was being sought for the King William Street site. The meteoric rise in City rents that had occurred made the prospect of a move rather frightening, but the firm was advised that in the circumstances it stood a good chance of getting an office development permit. And so it was that, in association with a major insurance company whose development could not otherwise get beyond the drawing board, a new building was erected on Finsbury Pavement with internal layout and fittings designed specially for the firm's needs.

The firm gained possession of the new offices in November 1971, taking the whole building except for the ground floor which became a banking hall. Fitting out work took some months, and the firm actually moved in over the Easter weekend of 1972.

The business environment in which the firm operated during this period was also hectic, full of large company mergers—and large company failures. Boom years in the City and in the economy gave way to years of intense financial stress, with marked swings in politics and government to make life doubly complicated. Here, one may pick out certain salient points in the progress of TMcL London. In 1965 came the Finance Act which introduced

Corporation Tax and Capital Gains Tax, the longest and most complex act for years, creating an enormous amount of work for all professional accountants. 1968 saw the merger with Martin Farlow & Co. In 1968 TMcL were asked to take on the audit and some special work for a large part of the Co-operative Wholesale Society. This was a major area of new work for the firm, one of the few new openings available at that time to the accountancy profession, and provided work in various centres, mainly Manchester.

In 1969 there came the first conference for all UK partners — a major step in the unification of the UK practice, and now a regular event. But the next year saw the failure of attempted unification in another sphere; as already told, the various professional organizations for accountants formally admitted failure in their efforts to integrate.

The year 1971 brought the first woman partner in the London firm's history, Mary Yale, a tax specialist and formerly a senior tax manager. The early 1970s was also a period of great expansion by a major client of TMcL, Grand Metropolitan. A series of successful take-over bids by Grand Met brought to TMcL the audit of groups like Express Dairy, Berni Inns, Mecca, Trumans and Watney Mann the brewers. Later Clifford Smith, a senior McLintock partner, left the firm to become finance director of Grand Met. The winter of 1973/74 brought the restrictions on use of electricity, caused by the miners' strike, and along with many others the firm had to get by with lighting on three days a week, staggered hours, and a lot of work done at home.

The year 1974 saw the appointment of ex-Marine, Major-General John Owen, as 'chef de cabinet' in London — an appointment more fully explained in the next chapter. One other appointment of interest, but in the reverse direction, was made that year. Michael Haines of TMcL joined the Department of Trade and Industry on secondment for two years, in accordance with a recently initiated government policy of bringing into the civil service people with business experience, to mirror the increasing involvement of government in industry.

If 1975 brought a rather down-beat note, with the decision, more fully explained elsewhere, to dissolve the consortium partnership with Whinney Murray in the management consultancy field, 1976 then brought a very definite up-beat note to the business. For apart from liquidation work and receiverships, particularly in connection with the unscrambling of several large property companies, TMcL were appointed auditors to two new government-created organizations, the National Enterprise Board and the British National Oil Corporation, both of them 'big' appointments offering the prospect of substantial work—in the case of the Oil Corporation in both Scotland and London.

This then, in necessarily brief form, brings the story as up to date as history may go. But to sustain the growth, in national coverage, in numbers and in business, that had taken place by the early 1970s, TMcL realized that it needed to take a new look at itself, at how it operated and was organized. That is the subject of the next chapter.

Chapter Eleven

ORGANIZE AND CONSENT

'For forms of government let fools contest;
Whate'er is best administered is best:'

(*Pope: 'An essay on Man' – Epistle III lines* 303 *&* 304)

(Quoted by Donald Ironside, one of the 'Three Wise Men' of the TMcL Steering Committee, in his report on the firm's organization in May 1974).

ALTHOUGH LONDON, because of its size and geographical location, is a natural focal point for many matters it is not the 'head office' of TMcL, a fact as readily accepted in London as elsewhere; indeed TMcL has no 'head office' in the generally accepted business use of the term. Instead, over recent years there has been increasing use of the descriptions 'region' and 'regional firm', and these at present are London, Birmingham, the north-west, the north-east, Bristol, East Midlands, Northern Ireland and Scotland. In each of these regions (and indeed in individual offices within the region) partners have autonomous powers in many matters; that is why the firm never uses the word 'branch' to describe any of them. On the other hand, clients and the public at large regard TMcL as a national firm, and it must provide an even quality of service (and of course a top quality service) throughout the UK. This means that there are many matters on which the collective best interest of TMcL is best served by unified action and approach.

This desire to combine a high degree of local autonomy with a high degree of cohesion explains the otherwise rather complicated-looking organization structure that has governed McLintocks since the beginning of 1975. This structure found its genesis in Donald Ironside's report of 1974. Ironside was then senior partner in the Bristol office, and his report stated bluntly:

'We have been so busy saying to ourselves that we value our personal and local autonomy and that we do not want to pool profits throughout the UK that our consciousness of being one firm has been at a very low level. That is not surprising; we are a federation and most federations have been slow (and often reluctant) to recognize their oneness.'

But that was changing, with the growing recognition that 'the partners of TMcL constitute one firm. Our oneness is based on our use of the name TMcL & Co and our commonality of purposes. We recognize that the act of a single partner or office may affect partners elsewhere in the UK and that there are some things which we can only do, or can do much more effectively, if we do them together rather than separately.'

It is, of course, significant, and consistent with the basic decentralized philosophy of McLintocks that it was the senior partner from Bristol, and not from either London, the largest office, or from Glasgow, the original office, who wrote this report and made the proposals that brought about the present administrative system of the firm. Probably only a non-Londoner and a non-founder could have gained approval for measures of centralization and standardization within the firm's federalist outlook; possibly also the problem was clearer when seen from Bristol, and the construction of a generally acceptable remedy easier. For Bristol was and is a large, independent-minded office in its own right, with strong traditions and habits of its own, determined to play at least its rightful part in the affairs of the firm as a whole from the day it joined TMcL in 1969. Bristol had also had previous experience of the problems of association with another firm.

Before the Ironside report, TMcL had been 'governed' simply and solely by its UK Policy Committee. This had already been re-organized once before, in 1972, as a result of a report by Sir William Slimmings, the senior partner in London. Previously it had consisted simply of senior partners from each office; from 1972 it became two partners from each office, on the grounds that the senior partner was not necessarily the best or only representative of the general feeling in his office. But there remained a deeper problem, that the committee as a whole lacked effectiveness; it had no means of getting its decisions translated into action, and the same topics tended to crop up again and again on its agenda.

So it came about that Ironside was commissioned to rethink the system from the beginning; in pursuit of a new pattern of self-government, he travelled round all the offices, talked to as many partners as he could (with, as he admits, a fairly clear idea already in his mind of what he was after), and produced his plan. The plan was in large part implemented, to produce the structure as it is now (and as it is shown diagrammatically at the end of this chapter). But at least as important as the plan itself was the frank diagnosis that went with it, which showed how important such self-analysis must be to a firm operating by consent and consensus rather than by command and coercion. Here is such an extract from Ironside's report:

'Within our commonality of purposes there are tensions which we need to recognize—between the wishes of our clients and the constraints imposed by law and by the institutes; between our desire to exercise individual judgment and entrepreneurial skill and the need to conform to "the firm's view"; between our view of partnership as a close personal relationship and the impossibility of such a relationship with every one of eighty or so partners; between our wish to be involved in running the firm and the need for a speedy decision-making process; between the kind of work we like best or think most socially useful and that which the firm needs us to do or which pays best; and even between our pride in the history and traditions of the firm and the recognition that we may need to merge sideways (or upwards?) with a firm with different traditions and habits if we are to continue to have the opportunity to do difficult and challenging work for large clients. As well as these tensions there are the differences that can be expected between partners of different age and temperament, even although they have grown up or have been absorbed into the firm's tradition of high professional competence. We need a style of government which will serve our common purposes and use the tensions and differences which are inherent in our situation in a constructive way.'

The report went on: 'Some partners have expressed to me disappointment at the slow progress which we are making in fashioning an appropriate style of government for the UK firm. We should remember that the task is an exceedingly difficult one; it is that of organizing a large number of people of above average intellectual capacity, each with the independence that comes from a professional training, so that they can make decisions or give advice to clients on matters of importance and difficulty, often in circumstances of considerable pressure and tension. This is much more difficult than managing a manufacturing firm many times our size.

'We should not assume that some of our more highly structured rivals are free of problems, not least that of attracting and retaining over a long period of time much needed people who are highly intelligent, welcome responsibility, are extremely effective in their professional work but do not easily conform to organizational norms. In some ways the problem is similar to that of managing scientific research.'

The report also fully recognized the virtues of the federal structure: 'Our strong out-of-London firms are a valuable and distinguishing feature of the firm. Our federal structure permits, within quite wide limits, different styles of government within our various firms in response to their traditions, to local circumstances, the personalities of local partners and the influence of national policies as they evolve. A highly structured, centrally directed and autocratic style of government is not readily compatible with a federal structure (particularly one comprising people engaged on professional work) so that it is not surprising that we reject it. Most partners (but not all) want to be involved in some measure in the management of the firm and all of us, I am sure, in taking major decisions. This leads us also to reject an oligarchic government.'

But—and this was the nub of the matter—'Partners recognize that there has to be some trade-off between participation, open government, consultation, persuasion and consensus-seeking on the one hand and efficiency, effectiveness, economy in the use of partners' time, discreet handling of personal issues and speed of decision on the others'.

What then should be done? There were, of course, several possible variants on the basic federal idea; for example, 'It would be possible to combine a federal structure with central pooling of profits which are then redistributed from the centre. That would tend to move some decisions away from regional firms to the UK Policy Committee. Several partners would be willing for this to be done but no one to whom I have spoken believes that we are yet ready as a firm to make such a change. Partners recognize that our arrangements lead to a situation where there may be quite a gap (and I do not mean simply a cost of living differential) between the earnings of partners who are of the same age and carrying much the same level of responsibility but who are in different offices. Several partners have mentioned the fact that in the absence of central pooling it is more difficult to get agreement about the financing of new national projects; but they are still not disposed to advocate a change.'

So central pooling of profits, that most tangible of all signs of a unified rather than a diversified structure, was rejected, at least for the time being.

But there remained the things that clearly needed to be done on a national basis. These Ironside listed as:

1 Things which are necessary for the protection of the good name of TMcL, eg inter-office inspection, conformity to the firm's view of technical issues, prescription of audit standards.

2 Things which can only be done together, eg a national merger, long-range planning for the firm as a whole.

3 Things which are better done or more economically done on a co-operative basis, eg training, technical memoranda.

The structure which he then suggested and which was in broad concept implemented, was that within the UK Policy Committee there should be a 'Steering Committee' of three men, partners from different offices but all commanding confidence throughout the firm, which would act as a focal point for all the main concerns of the UKPC, and which would give to the UKPC the status, cohesion and influence which it then lacked.

Secondly, answering to the UKPC, there should be a series of executive committees, one for each main topic area—audit, taxation, training, finance, liquidations, inter-office inspection, and so on. In addition, there should be a nominations committee to put up names for membership of these executive committees. Last, but by no means least, there should be a secretariat, answerable to the Steering Committee, charged with the job of either implementing, or monitoring the implementation of, the decisions taken by the UKPC and the Steering Committee. This secretariat would be headed by John Owen, himself one of the more unique features of McLintocks. A former major-general of the

Royal Marines, he was recruited originally as 'chef de cabinet' of the London office, in recognition of the growing complexity of simply managing a large accountancy business, but with half an eye on the role which he might in due course play for the firm as a whole—both in its management and organization, and in internal and external communications.

One interesting point is the size of the executive committees and the Steering Committee—all made up of only three men each. In his report, Ironside pointed out that there was 'a general dislike of "committee government", a preference for assigning specified functions and tasks to people who will get things done, a recognition of the importance of good communications (and of the risk of swamping the message in too big a volume of paper) and acceptance of the necessity for a limit on the amount of time which partners spend on non chargeable work'.

On the other hand, it was extremely difficult to take away individual partners or managers full time from their work.

'I have asked each of the regional firms if they are willing to release a partner to work virtually full time on such administrative and similar work. A certain number of partners are in favour of doing this but no firm is willing to release a partner for the purpose and each gives convincing reasons for their refusal.'

The compromise arrived at was the number of three.

'My preference for three stems from my feeling that:

'1 A one-person "group" is not suitable because there is too little check on judgments made, and on under—or over—activity.

'2 In a pair there is a risk that one person dominates or, alternatively, there can be difficulty in resolving differences.

'3 In a troika (three abreast) there is a better chance of proposals being weighed and assessed in a consensus forming atmosphere.

'A troika will also often provide the opportunity to involve partners from more than one office. I do not, of course, expect that each group will necessarily itself do the whole of the work (or even the thinking, to make a somewhat false distinction!) that has to be done in its own area.'

In practice, the three-man executive groups have tended, like the Steering Committee itself, to comprise one London representative, one from Glasgow, and one from the other regional offices; but there has been a deliberate policy to keep a large proportion of the chairmanships of these committees in the hands of non-London, non-Glasgow people, again to promote the federal all-are-basically-equal idea.

The Steering Committee from its inception consisted similarly of Sir William Slimmings from London, John Kirkpatrick from Glasgow, and (hardly surprisingly) Donald Ironside himself from Bristol.

How then does the structure actually work? This is how Bill Morrison, joint senior partner in Glasgow, summarized it soon after it was put into being:

'1 The powers of the UK Policy Committee are in essence powers of persuasion and guidance rather than powers of instruction and direction, and it provides a "high level" sounding board for all matters of importance to the firm. It is fair to say that no matter agreed by the UK Policy Committee has failed to be implemented throughout the regions.

'2 The Steering Committee sees to the implementation of the policies laid down by the UKPC and agreed to by the regions, progress chases and directs the efforts of the executive groups and deals with *ad hoc* matters affecting the firm as a whole which require action between UKPC meetings; it will be noted that the joint chairmen of the UKPC and of the Steering Committee are the same two people—Sir William Slimmings and Mr Kirkpatrick.

'3 Apart from the Finance Group, who deal with common TMcL & Co costs, inter-office time rates and the like, it will be seen that all the executive groups deal either with personnel and training or with technical matters. The personnel group is concerned with the longer and wider aspects of human resources, and does not conflict with the staff partners in each office or with their own *ad hoc* committee; training continues, and will no doubt expand upon the services already provided in this area since 1969. Inter-office inspection continues, and the other groups formalize and intensify the study of technical subjects and the preparation of related literature.

'4 The UKPC Executive Secretariat is headed by Mr John Owen who is secretary to the London partnership, to the UKPC, to the Steering Committee, and in McLintock Main Lafrentz, to the Eastern Executive Committee and jointly to the Board of Management. Not being an accountant, he brings an air of objectivity and perspective to what the firm does, and is the focal point for much of the exchange of information within the firm.'

UNITED KINGDOM ORGANIZATION

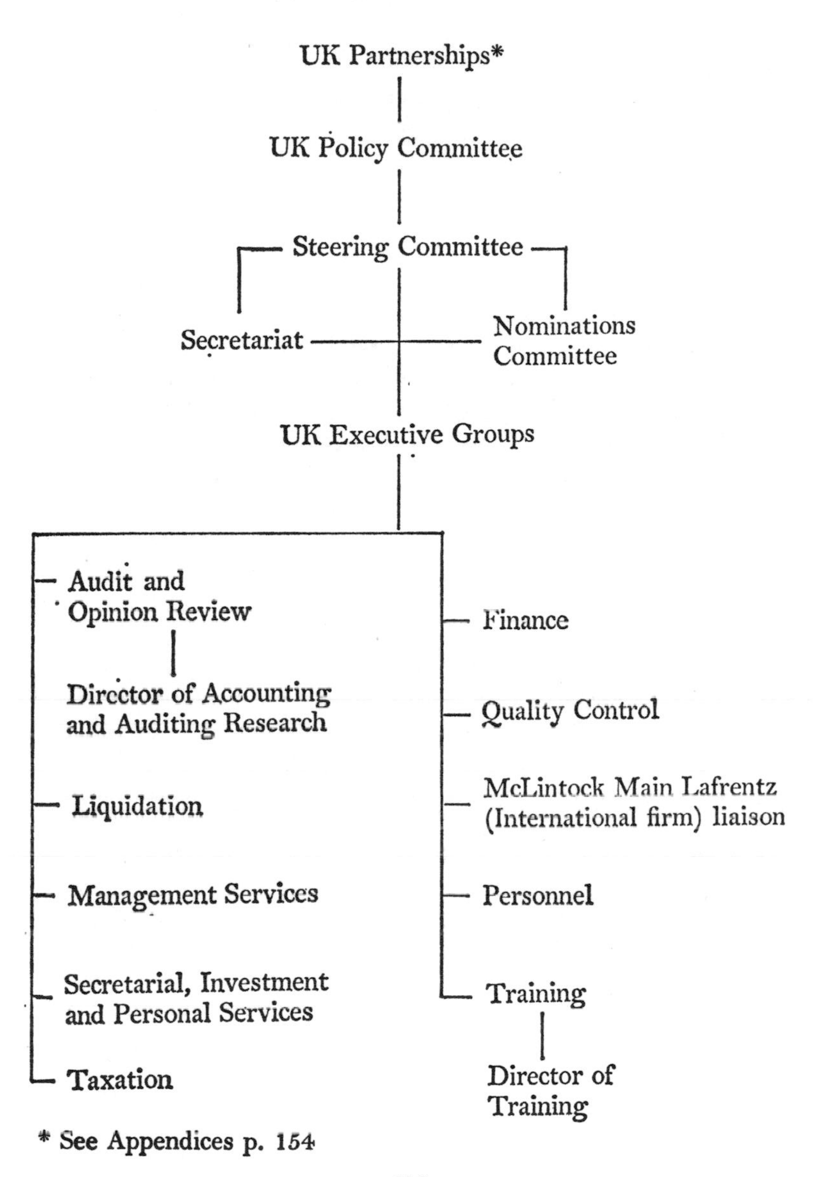

* See Appendices p. 154

Chapter Twelve

LOOKING AFTER ITS PEOPLE

THE ULTIMATE touchstone of any organization, but especially of one like Thomson McLintock & Co which prides itself on being an intensely personal firm, must be the way in which it looks after its people. To show what lies behind the organization charts and growth trees of TMcL we may take two of the more personal aspects of the firm – one conventionally labelled 'social and welfare' and dating right back to the days of the firm's founder; the other an ultra-contemporary activity and necessity of the firm if it is to attract and keep good people, 'training'.

Social and Welfare

In 1913, when TC Guthrie entered in the Glasgow office, Thomson McLintock 'seemed to regard his staff as next to the members of his family and paid bonuses and holiday money to all his staff when no other firm in Glasgow that I knew did.'

The weddings of members of the McLintock family were great occasions. Guthrie was present at two such marriages and 'on both wedding evenings Thomson McLintock entertained the whole staff to dinner and the theatre and attended with his wife. Even one poor soul on the staff who could not keep off the bottle was treated with great sympathy and tolerance.'

The reputation of McLintocks as generous employers

was carefully guarded, and bonus schemes have been in operation in Glasgow since before the first world war.

From the earliest days 'all the McLintocks were very good employers, always willing to give help to any of their staff in trouble or distress'. This tradition has been maintained to the present day, though, through time, formal bonus arrangements and a compulsory, contributory staff pension scheme have been evolved. In London for many years all the staff received a bonus of 10% plus £10 holiday money, Sir William McLintock's aim being that staff did take a proper holiday. With the introduction of PAYE in 1943 the holiday money disappeared and the amount was amalgamated with the general bonus. Each year the partners make recommendations on all the staff in their department on a good, bad or indifferent basis and these reports are also taken as a guide for salary increases. There is no minimum period for staff to qualify for a bonus, indeed those who have only worked for part of a year receive a proportion. The bonus is paid out in good years and bad and is a charge on the accounts before net profits.

In the London office the excellent restaurant and the pension scheme are both subsidized by the firm. Widows of members of the staff and elderly pensioners in difficulty are willingly helped. For example, a retired employee of over eighty and in failing health got into financial trouble. Eventually, a welfare officer traced the firm through the superannuation fund and rang up to discuss the problem. There were debts outstanding; but matters could be sorted out with the help of the welfare officer. It was arranged that a cheque should be sent at once to clear the debts and the pension was then re-arranged in such a way that the old man could manage.

The widows of partners have always been carefully looked after and in many cases their affairs are run by the firm. In the early years, there were a considerable number of comfortably situated but financially helpless people, often widows with small estates. These were in effect run by

Thomson McLintock & Co and many aspects of their lives were dealt with.

There is a long tradition of money being allocated for charity. In Sir William's day, considerable sums were sent direct to institutions and concerns which interested him particularly. These were mainly boys' clubs and the various children's charities, which in those days depended largely on voluntary subscriptions. Since the second world war, the State has increasingly covered this field and these beneficiaries have been taken off the firm's list. Nowadays, the firm has a deed of covenant with the National Council of Social Services. A list of the donations required by the firm is given to the National Council, who then make the allocation, recovering tax at the standard rate. The list reflects the special interests of the partners and is reviewed and kept up to date from time to time. Generally, a sum is kept in hand for any special disaster appeal, such as relief in an area devastated by earthquake or tornado.

The London office dinner, first held in 1918, is now a fairly regular event. On 14 March 1964 a special dinner and dance was held to celebrate the fiftieth anniversary of the London office. On that occasion a £10 gift token was given to all members of the staff and gold watches were presented to all those who had done twenty years' service or more. The presentation of gold watches to all staff with twenty years' service has become a regular custom.

Within the London office there are numerous extra-mural activities. There are sports teams and football, cricket and golf are played. Matches take place with other firms, between offices (there is an annual cricket match with the Birmingham office), and, in the case of golf, between partners and staff. The office has a choir and each year a carol service is held in a nearby church attended by large numbers of the employees of Thomson McLintock & Co, partners' wives and children and former members of the staff, children of the staff and a wide circle of friends.

An outsider entering the door of McLintocks' office in

London would be struck by the friendly atmosphere; staff at all levels are unfailingly helpful. The place is a hive of activity, but the people radiate an unusual degree of warmth, a fact which would no doubt please the shades of Thomson McLintock and his son William who cared so much for their staff.

In Glasgow, as in London, staff problems are sorted out, pensioners in difficulty are looked after and sums are allocated to charity. The tradition of the annual office party in Glasgow has always been maintained. A dinner-dance is held, attended by partners and their wives, partners from other Thomson McLintock offices and all staff accompanied by a guest. These occasions are much enjoyed.

The atmosphere of friendliness extends to the cleaning staff, many of whom have been with the firm for years and the jobs are handed down from mother to daughter. The standard of their work is noticeably high.

The Glasgow office, with its roots stretching back into history, has a very special atmosphere. This is a priceless asset, and it is to be hoped that growth and the demands of modern business do not force too much change. West George Street is beautiful, if not a little inconvenient, and it is full of character. The shades of Thomson McLintock himself lurk there.

Training

The reason why training sits easily with 'social welfare' as part of the 'people concern' of Thomson McLintock is that the firm views training as also a social activity, a chance to meet and talk with staff from other offices of the firm, so helping to strengthen that network of personal relationships that is the essential 'glue' to its federal organization structure. This view of training means that the firm uses hotels and universities for its courses, to provide a pleasing environment, and holds courses all over the country, rather than at one central training centre in London, the object being to ensure that staff from all offices get roughly equal access to the training programme. The firm tries to ensure a reasonable mix of people from its various areas, and the schedule shows courses held as far apart as Inverness-shire, in Scotland, and Devon, in the south of England. This is, as the firm puts it, 'an optimum budget rather than a minimum budget' approach, but its logic is clear enough. For the same reason, that of welding together the TMcL federation, the training programme was the first collective activity to get off the ground once the firm had assumed more or less its present shape in the UK in 1969/70.

The firm allocates a regular proportion of gross income to training, with (from 1976) two full-time training officers. Training is an expensive activity, and its cost was one of the factors which caused a number of firms to decide to throw in their lot with a larger grouping like Thomson McLintock & Co.

So far, the training courses have been mainly aimed at the audit side, though with some attention to taxation in the light of new legislation. Audit is of course a particular attraction to new recruits to the firm, and the training philosophy is to be selective in what is taught (ie special problems) rather than an across-the-board approach. The firm uses the more specialized courses run by the accountancy institutes in Scotland and England to supplement its own programme, and some members of the firm attend language courses and business school. This last reflects the growing and inevitable interest of TMcL in the art and practice of management itself, as the task of managing the firm gets more complex. This interest is also reflected in the use made of the Scottish Institute's course for 'young executives', and in the management courses started in 1976 by the firm itself.

This is one reason why the aim is to send most people on a course of some sort each year, and the number of course participants has been reaching over 800 per year, or about a half the total complement, even allowing for some people taking two courses. There are also some overseas students from McLintock Main Lafrentz, especially on the audit case study courses. MML has its own training arrangements, the essence of which is to teach the auditing of multi-national companies. Their accounts must be produced under overseas reporting requirements, and this means that auditing of their various activities must be done in a standard way. One means of achieving this is to send people abroad, and what MML and TMcL have done is to develop training modules which each separate office of the MML federation can use itself for in-house training. Each firm has to handle its own training as far as possible, using these modules, and the main MML training effort as such lies in teaching people how to use the modules.

But for TMcL itself, training is one of those aspects where an increasingly national view has been taken of the firm's requirements, through the medium of the relevant sub-committees of the UK Policy Committee; it quickly became the first common thread of the national firm, and is one of the main instruments in unifying the procedures and practices of the firm.

Chapter Thirteen

THE INTERNATIONAL IDEA

A STATEMENT of the philosophy lying behind the development of McLintock Main Lafrentz, the international organization through which Thomson McLintock went 'truly international' in the 1960s was given to the ninth international meeting of MML, held in September 1974 in Killarney, Ireland. The author was James M Halsey, a partner in the US firm of Main Lafrentz, who had by then spent ten years in professional and administrative work for the international firm. This is what he said:

'The philosophy which has created and bound together the multi-national association of professional firms known as McLintock Main Lafrentz is that the best service can be rendered to multi-national clients of our group by strong national firms staffed by competent national professionals. Our objectives are to provide clients locally and at their headquarters not only with the professional services expected of a modern accounting firm, but also with competent knowledge of the prevailing economic, social and fiscal conditions in each country.

'This philosophy rejects the proposition that a world-wide professional organization must be dominated by one firm of a particular nationality or that staff in foreign locations must be dominated by expatriates. Further, because the initial monetary resources of the founding firms of MML were limited, our association had to comprise only national firms that were economically viable on their own in their country. No firm in our group, therefore, should be economically dependent on international referred work for its survival.

'Since economic considerations, though important, are not vital, the real requirement of members of the MML group is one of attitude—a realization and acceptance of the premise that our profession must be practised on an international level and that our clients must be served in accordance with certain basic standards as well as those laid down by referring national firms.

'To establish and maintain the highest standards for accounting, auditing, management advisory, tax and related services, MML now provides training programmes, professional material, specialized assistance, personnel transfers and quality control for all members of the group. MML has grown steadily in coverage and in strength and is increasingly known as a major world-wide professional organization.'

While comparisons may be invidious, the full significance of this philosophy may be best brought out by contrasting it with the very different philosophy outlined in the history of another international firm, published when that firm was fifty years old in 1963. In that book there is a chapter headed, bluntly, 'Strengthening the One-Firm Concept'. A passage from this chapter reads:

'The secret of building a firm rather than an association of individual practices lies in establishing and maintaining a "one-firm" concept to such a degree that it will override and take precedence over the basic tendency that is always present to operate independently'. The chapter then goes on to speak in terms of 'strong centralized management', 'speaking with one voice on accounting principles', 'centralized control of recruiting', and 'standardization of personnel policies', with a full line management organization and formal rules for delegation of authority. Clearly, nothing could be further from the concept adopted by either TMcL itself within the UK, or by McLintock Main Lafrentz internationally.

How MML arrived at its particular philosophy was excellently put by Bill Morrison, joint senior partner in Glasgow, in a talk to the TMcL audit managers conference in Banbury later in 1974.

'There are three principal ways to form an international accounting organization:

(a) Open up offices all over the world in your own name, with your own personnel
(b) Operate purely on a correspondent/representative basis
(c) Set up a federation of national firms.

'When in 1964/65, it was clear that TMcL & Co had to formalize its international position there were two reasons, as I understand it, why (c) was the chosen format. Firstly we were years and years behind certain others in category (a) which would have been, in any event, prohibitively expensive to copy; and secondly we believed solidly in the philosophy of category (c), having really outgrown category (b). The tremendous growth of referred work, work retained which would otherwise have been lost, and work acquired from category (a) and (b) firms, all point to our international philosophy having been correct from inception.

'What was that philosophy? It has always been, and was recently confirmed yet again as, the philosophy that MML should comprise a federation of leading national firms operating—for international purposes—under the MML banner. In this way member firms can continue to operate their national practices with complete autonomy, while servicing the needs of multi-national clients. This is to ensure that strong national firms with local knowledge of legal, tax, and accounting requirements, and a range of good contacts are available to international clients. With increasing nationalistic tendencies in recent years the foresight of our predecessors has proved invaluable.'

As Morrison candidly pointed out, there was a very

practical reason behind the adoption of this 'federalist' philosophy; or perhaps not one reason, but a cluster of related reasons. Neither McLintocks itself in the UK nor Main Lafrentz in the US were or are among the very biggest national firms; and as Halsey mentioned in his statement, financial resources were limited. This in itself indicated a need to link with already established overseas firms. But one reason why neither firm was or is among the biggest in its country is precisely because, as Morrison mentions, they were late in the day in opening up offices abroad. The published histories of two other firms give the following dates for the opening of their various offices: in one case—Paris 1920, Brussels and Antwerp 1924, Rome 1923, Milan 1927, Vienna and Berlin 1927 (both later closed), Buenos Aires and other South American offices 1912 and the years following, Johannesburg and other South African offices 1906, New York 1890, and other US offices later: in the other case—Brussels 1921, Paris 1930, Antwerp 1948, Rotterdam 1949, Johannesburg 1931, Rhodesia and East Africa 1947–54, Australia and New Zealand 1948, Canada 1936, New York 1926. One may contrast the position of Thomson McLintock in the early 1960s with an office in Lisbon from 1965, associations with a few continental firms—and an office in Paris that opened and closed within a few years in the early 1930s.

Whether this comparative neglect of international business before the 1960s simply reflects the late start of Thomson McLintock as a firm, or whether it mirrors the disinterest in overseas business of Sir William McLintock, the man who in effect guided the firm's destinies from 1920 to 1947, may be a matter of argument. The already quoted remark of Sir William that, 'It is bad enough men signing my name in Birmingham and Paris, but never in Buenos Aires' must however confirm the view that, had Sir William's outlook been more international, the problem that faced McLintocks in the 1960s in creating an international coverage might have been easier. For it meant that in that post-war period, when other accountancy firms were hectically expanding, or building on previous expansion, McLintocks had little to go on.

The US firm of Main Lafrentz was in much the same position, as was explained to the 1974 MML meeting:

'Generally, our colleagues in the international field were well established organizations of the Big 8 (of the USA), some of which had been implanted as much as seventy years earlier. The amount of money available to our founding firms to invest in an international organization was limited and could not possibly approach the vast sums that had been expended by major accounting firms who "went international" since world war II.'

In that sense, the creation of MML in the 1960s was essentially a catching-up operation, with a strong defensive element to it. To call it 'defensive' is not to minimize its achievement; but as with tax work, an international organization is these days one of those things which, if you have not got it, is liable to lose you clients to firms who have got it. The 1974 meeting was told:

'The United States firm found itself in a serious competitive position in view of the fact that most of the overseas work of its major clients was being dealt with by colleague firms who frequently used their international connections as a practice development tool in the United States.'

In other words, in the very severe competitive climate of the US accountancy business, the US firms which were auditing the overseas subsidiaries of Main Lafrentz's biggest US clients (Main Lafrentz having at that time very limited overseas representation), might have used this as a way of trying to attract these clients away from Main Lafrentz in respect of their domestic US auditing work as well. It is no secret, therefore, that the first initiative and main initial drive for an international organization came from the US firm. But this initiative met with a ready response from many partners in the UK firm (not, at first, from all) and it was not long before the overseas expansion of some of McLintocks' own UK clients, in particular Grand Metropolitan Hotels, demonstrated the equal need for the UK firm to have an international organization, if only for these selfsame 'defensive' reasons.

To be fair to those who were sceptical at first, there were and are drawbacks to MML's philosophy of organization. 'There are three main ones', declared Morrison in 1974. 'Not all staff speak English, and as the bulk of work is referred from English-speaking countries this can cause one or two problems. Secondly, the dual concept of national firms acting as an international firm makes it more difficult to get the international name known in all countries (because the national firm continues to deal with its own clients in its own name). Thirdly, the differences in practices and procedures, and sometimes even in objectives, are wide, although of course each firm is "top drawer" in its own country. This serves to emphasize the need for international manuals, training programmes, personnel exchanges, and, naturally, communications.'

He went on to mention a fourth reason that has worried some partners. 'MML is a conscious loss-maker, the loss representing development costs, or international investment.' MML's income is a nominal administrative contribution levied on fees deriving from referred work between member firms and its costs are those of supporting certain key countries, quality control, staff relocation, operating its executive and technical committees, producing manuals, holding the annual conference, and so forth.

The loss is not large—about $100,000 in 1973/74 and $50,000 in 1974/75—but there must be substantial hidden costs in terms of people's time taken up in the administration of MML. Nevertheless, the quantified and unquantified costs of MML are, as Morrison says, a type of investment in the future. They ultimately derive from another basic tenet of the philosophy of MML, as expressed at the 1974 meeting: 'Our founders were determined that MML should not be a weak, paper organization comprised of correspondent relationships susceptible of no supervision of standards and therefore fraught with danger.'

In other words, such drawbacks as there are arise from the basic nature of the philosophy adopted in creating MML, and are more properly regarded as the price of its demonstrable success. For, as Halsey said: 'Our founders devised a means of operating that appeals to professional men, and a flexibility of organization which makes MML acceptable in many countries which are presently taking a very hostile view of international accounting firms. With our philosophy, our friendship and professional respect for one another, MML is closing the gap that existed between it and our larger and once better-known colleagues.

'Armed with this philosophy, our founders set out to find the best like-minded unattached firms in various countries with the idea that each firm joining the MML group would henceforth have two identities—their local national name for their continuing local practice and the MML name for their international practice.'

How they set about this task is the subject of the next chapter.

Chapter Fourteen

THE MML STORY

THE INTERNATIONAL organization known as McLintock Main Lafrentz was set up in late 1964 by Thomson McLintock & Co, Martin Farlow & Co of London (who later merged with TMcL) and Main Lafrentz & Co of the US. These initial partners were shortly joined by Riddell Stead & Co (now Thorne Riddell & Co) of Canada and subsequently by Pelser, Hamelberg, van Til & Co of Holland, and Hancock Woodward & Neill* of Australia; these five firms, together with Julien H Fayet, the first individual international partner, constitute the present partners of McLintock Main Lafrentz – International. This is not a practising firm, but acts as a co-ordinating body, taking responsibility for professional standards, practice development, communications and administration throughout the organization. The practising firm is McLintock Main Lafrentz & Co, which has, amongst other things, more individual international partners.

The first seeds of what was to become MML are to be found in a letter dated 5 August 1963 from a partner in the Pittsburgh firm of Main and Company to the UK firm of Brown, Fleming and Murray. In that letter he explained both the imminent merger of Main & Co with FW Lafrentz & Co, and the unsatisfactory nature of the overseas arrangements of the merged firm. This is what he said:

'Negotiations for the merging of our firm with FW Lafrentz & Co, a sizeable USA national firm, are approaching consummation. While they are two-thirds our size, their

* now Hancock & Offner.

clients have far more subsidiaries abroad than we do.

'The combined firm, to be named Main Lafrentz & Co, will have initially twenty-one offices in the US, and will involve accounting problems outside the US. These are now being handled by approximately fifty different public accounting firms. I am not in a position to estimate the volume of work involved—as in many cases the fees are paid directly by the client to the foreign accounting firm.

'We are not pleased with the manner in which this work is spread. It appears disjointed and certainly will be difficult to supervise. In many cases we must assume responsibility for the work of the other accountants. Also, it is evident that some of these clients want the work done under our name, in some fashion or other.

'In view of the magnitude of this problem, I should like to arrange a personal discussion with you, in London, and whomever else you may wish to have present during the week of 23 September 1963.'

A reply from a partner in Brown, Fleming and Murray in September says, among other things, 'I have made preliminary arrangements with Thomson McLintock on the footing that they would entertain you for lunch on Monday. . . .'

So we see the entry of McLintocks into the negotiations —from which Brown, Fleming and Murray later dropped out. The explanation of how McLintocks and Martin Farlow came into the picture as they did, and how the other founding partners came to be there, is rather complicated.

FW Lafrentz & Co had actually established an association with Martin Farlow as early as 1908. (Lafrentz had also established relationships with the Argentinean firm of Carlos E Ackerman y Asociados and the Mexican firm of Despacho Rodolfo Hernandez in the early sixties.) Main & Co, the other predecessor of Main Lafrentz, had earlier established, together with Thomson McLintock and Brown Fleming and Murray, McLintock Murray Main & Co to deal with the North American work of the two UK partners. Thomson McLintock & Co had earlier working relationships with the predecessors of Pelser, Hamelberg, van Til & Co as well as with Fides Treuhandgesellschaft in North Germany and working arrangements of many years with the South African firm of Alex Aiken & Carter. Martin Farlow had also worked with a number of European firms prior to the founding of MML.

McLintocks had also had a joint firm in Canada, again with Brown, Fleming and Murray, operated in conjunction with Sharpe Milne of Canada, a not very successful venture which did, however, bring them into contact with Main. It followed, therefore, that McLintocks was one of the two London firms that Main would naturally approach, while it was Martin Farlow that Lafrentz would naturally approach.

With the dropping out of Brown, Fleming and Murray and the later merger of Martin Farlow into McLintocks, the rather tangled skein of relationships sorted itself out into the recognizable pattern of today.

The decision that the firm should be established was actually taken in June 1964 when the newly merged Main Lafrentz had its own first all-partners meeting in Pocono Manor, USA. Four non-Americans attended this meeting —including James Macnair of TMcL and Leonard Treen of Martin Farlow. It was at this meeting, after much good-natured wrangling, that the McLintock Main Lafrentz name emerged. The first deed of partnership which established McLintock Main Lafrentz & Co was signed on 25 March 1965, and provided for the firm to begin operations on 1 April of that year. What enabled MML to get started so quickly was precisely that there were a number of pre-existing associations which could be built on and formalized.

By coincidence the TMcL branch office in Lisbon was also opened in 1965. The development of this office has an interesting history. Calouste Gulbenkian, who died in July 1955, having created the Gulbenkian Foundation in June 1953 based in Lisbon, requested in his will that Thomson McLintock should continue to look after his affairs. The establishment of an office in Lisbon resulted directly from this.

The first world directory was published in October 1965, six months after the founding of MML. Besides the United States and Britain, MML firms were by then established in Canada, Mexico, France, Germany, Portugal, Sweden, Switzerland, Argentina, Peru and Australia—twelve countries. At that time, Pelser, Hamelberg, van Til, although remaining a correspondent firm because of the regulations of the Dutch Institute, were very much a part of the family.

In the early years MML sought to maintain coverage in many areas through correspondent or representative ties. But the proportion of its coverage dealt with by representatives has declined with the continued establishment of MML firms in additional countries. By 1976 the MML group had grown to thirty-seven firms operating from two hundred and thirty offices in thirty-nine countries. It was still served by eleven representative firms operating from forty-nine offices in twenty-five countries, principally in East Africa and South-East Asia.

Not all of the original MML family of 1965 has remained in it. The original Canadian representation was a group of four firms which eventually divided while attempting to fulfil an earlier intention to amalgamate into one firm. So from 1 April 1968 Riddell Stead Graham and Hutchison, a predecessor firm to Thorne Riddell & Co, joined MML and became one of the partner firms to the underlying agreement. At the same time the combination of the practices of Martin Farlow and Thomson McLintock was accomplished and the new parties to the agreement continuing MML were Thomson McLintock, Main Lafrentz and Riddell Stead Graham and Hutchison.

On 1 July 1970 the Australian firm of Hancock Woodward & Neill replaced the firm of Cox Johnston & Co. Again the reason for the change was the failure of a group of Australian firms to maintain one national practice. Hancock Woodward & Neill were able to provide such a national practice and from 1 April 1973 became a party to the underlying agreement along with Pelser, Hamelberg, van Til who, by a modification of the regulations of the Dutch Institute, at last found themselves able formally to join MML.

A few other firms have come and gone in the MML organization—Revisionsfirmaet H Hjerno Jeppesen in Denmark, Loudon Blomquist & Co in Brazil, Estudio CR Leon Buka in Uruguay and 'Consulta' SL in Colombia. In 1974 the association of several years with the Sao Paulo, Brazil, firm of Instituto Nacional de Auditores was replaced with the multi-office Brazilian firm of Walter Heuer, Contadores Auditores.

Early in 1975 the Eastern Executive of MML decided to find MML representatives in Nigeria, being the wealthiest and largest of the West African states, and in Iran. Negotiating teams went to those countries and were able to persuade substantial national firms—ZO Ososanya & Co of Lagos and Ibadan and Amin & Co of Teheran—to join MML. Partners from both these firms attended the 1975 MML conference in Amsterdam. In the Western Hemisphere* new arrangements were made with Pickenhayn y Asociados in Argentina and MML-Hong Kong was established with the existing MML representative John P Byrne & Co. Most important in the Western Hemisphere has been the establishment of MML-Japan with the national firm of Sanwa Tokyo Marunouchi and Co, which provides exclusive representation through the MML offices at Tokyo, Osaka and Fukuoki.

Within their own countries the MML firms include both the largest national firms, as in Canada and Panama, and some very small ones. All, however, share the common philosophy. A rough estimate indicates that the combined billings of all the member firms of MML exceeds $200,000,000. The broad pattern is, therefore, that other firms join with the five principal firms in two ways:

(a) As member firms—leading firms in many countries using the name MML, the stationery of MML and signing as MML.

* The terms Western and Eastern hemisphere are designatory to the areas which are so defined for administrative convenience in the international firm.

(b) As representative firms who for various reasons, such as that they do not yet wish total commitment, or that their country does not allow international firms to form there, cannot become full MML members. These display the representation on their letterhead, and perhaps at their door, but do not sign MML.

As time progressed and the international practice developed, it became necessary to devote more and more time to its administration. After more than two years in development, an administrative manual for MML was produced in late 1969 and updated in 1972 and again in 1976.

Then came the provision in the MML-International and MML & Co agreements of 1 April 1973 for active McLintock Main Lafrentz partners. Such active partners, to be differentiated from the representatives of the constituent firms, have only a single allegiance to MML. Not only does this provide a career opportunity in the international firm for qualified and deserving young men, but it also provides a further unifying force of professional men available to guide and assist all member firms.

As explained, MML-I is a non-practising firm, and MML & Co is the practising entity. It has three partners at present. These are Julien Fayet, the senior, ex-Riddell Stead partner and former president of the Quebec Institute, formerly based in Geneva, but now in Brussels; Anthony Smith, based in Brussels, but with former experience in Paris, New York, and London, where he trained with Martin Farlow; and Arthur Hunt, now in Brazil, who has MML experience in Lisbon, New York and Peru. These three men are full-time partners of MML operating in the field, and the number of international partners is expected to increase. A number of other people in the world-wide MML organization are working in countries other than those in which they began life.

But clearly far more than that was needed to bind together such a large collection of once quite separate and still totally autonomous firms. Inevitably, conferences became a fundamental part of the system, providing not only discussion and agreement on technical and professional issues, but also that cementing of personal relationships that must in the end be the binding force of an organization which much like the UK organization of Thomson McLintock itself only more so, quite deliberately lacks anything like a 'command structure'. The annual conference of MML has therefore become something of an institution—time-consuming and expensive no doubt, but irreplaceable.

The first annual conference was in June 1966, in Miami Beach, and was brought to a fitting end by the arrival of a hurricane. Apart from a lot of 'getting to know you' work, important organizational steps were taken. It was decided to publish a world directory, and most importantly the basic technical committees were established—accounting and auditing, then called accounting practices and procedures; taxation; management services; personnel and training, and investigations and mergers. At that time the idea of a policy committee had not been put forward, and the initial operational group of nine men was referred to as the executive committee.

The second international meeting took place in Cambridge, England in September 1967. It was at the Cambridge meeting that the executive committee became the policy committee and the New York and London administrations were named as executive arms of it. A first draft of the administration manual, which was finally published in 1969, was presented. For the first time there was a guest speaker, Mr Victor McDougall, the secretary of the Scottish Institute. This meeting also marked the first year of technical committee activity. Personnel and training had been the most active, especially in encouraging the attendance of staff from other countries at the training courses of Main Lafrentz and Thomson McLintock. The tax committee had organized itself into Eastern and Western Hemisphere sub-committees and had nominated tax liaison representatives in each national firm. At this meeting, the principles emerged that there should be annual meetings of MML, and the insurance coverage of MML was discussed. Eighty-two partners attended the Cambridge meeting; besides the UK, there were representatives from twenty countries and twenty-one different firms.

The third international meeting was held in New Jersey in the United States in June 1968. Besides the eighty-four general partners of Main Lafrentz, there were forty-one people from other countries, and eighteen firms and countries were represented. At this meeting the first combined financial statements of MML-International were presented. The combination of practices of Martin Farlow and Thomson McLintock was announced. The audit familiarization guide which had been developed in Europe for the European firms was reviewed by the accounting and auditing committee and shortly thereafter put into use. This guide served as a point of departure for the committee's later development of an audit manual. This was the last international meeting which was paid for directly by one of the underwriting firms. It was decided that henceforth they should be paid for by MML itself.

The fourth international meeting took place in Quebec City in September 1969. There was a total attendance of seventy-three of which fifty-nine were other-than-host-country. At this meeting the accounting and auditing committee was authorized to prepare an audit manual for MML, and the final draft of an administrative manual was approved. The personnel and training committee undertook to develop the MML training programme which was finally first presented in Holland before the 1971 annual conference. The personnel and training committee also raised the proposition 'whether there is now, or will be in the next few years, a role for personnel who will look to MML for their long-term career. This concept implies positions of manager and partner status within MML'. At this meeting referral fees, renamed administrative contributions, were standardized on a world-wide basis.

The fifth international meeting took place in Scotland in

Verum House – London office since 1972

BOARD ROOM

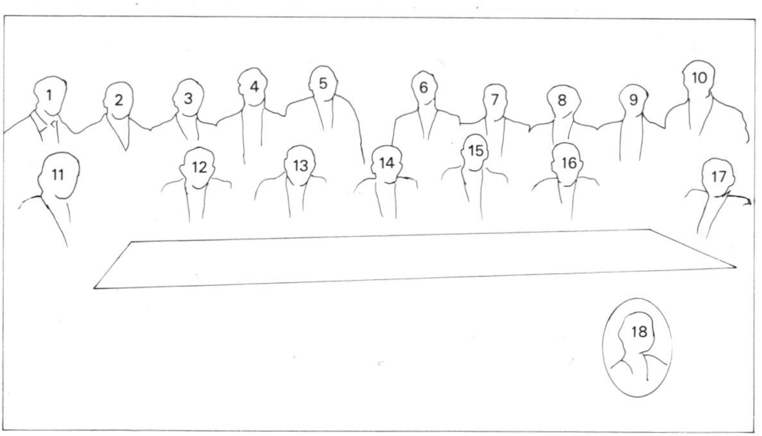
1
2
3
4
5
6
7
8
9
10
11
12
13
14
15
16
17
18

Thomson McLintock & Co
United Kingdom Policy
Committee – July 1976

1 Gordon S Lowden (alternate for Donald B Grant)
2 John Constantine (alternate for Henry M Pritchard)
3 David M Parkes
4 Martin G Adamson (alternate for James T H Macnair)
5 John H Golcher
6 Ian G Watt
7 Steven L Henderson
8 Peter J Artt
9 John Norris
10 John I H Owen (Secretary)
11 William McLaughlin
12 William Morrison
13 John L Kirkpatrick (Co-chairman)
14 Sir William Slimmings (Co-chairman)
15 Donald J Ironside
16 C Alan McLintock
17 William J M Alexander
18 (*inset*) Henry M Pritchard

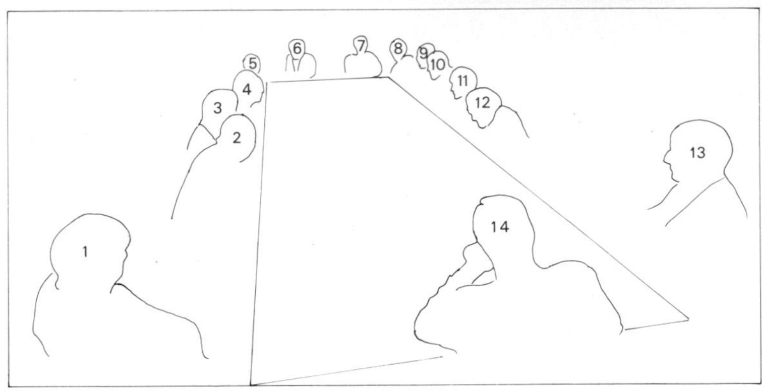

McLintock Main Lafrentz & Co Board of Management – March 1976

1 Kurt Reiner (Germany)
2 Julien H Fayet (MML & Co)
3 Sten Karlgren (Sweden)
4 LeRoy Layton (Chairman)
5 Charles W Neill (Australia) (alternate to J Arnold Hancock)
6 Antonio R Buron Jr (Panama)
7 Gerard F Westendorp (Holland)
8 Kenneth S Gunning (Canada)
9 John L Kirkpatrick (United Kingdom)
10 Archibald E MacKay (United States)
11 Lionel P Kent (Canada)
12 James T H Macnair (United Kingdom)
13 John I H Owen (Joint Secretary – London)
14 James M Halsey (Joint Secretary – New York)

Absent:

Cesareo Alonso G (Peru)
Pierre Gilot (France)
Charles F Toewe (United States)

October 1970. The functions and efficiency of the technical committees were reviewed, and there was criticism of the delay in their work, particularly of the MML training programme which should have had a pilot presentation immediately before the conference, but had to be postponed. The tax committee, however, had named its liaison representatives and was able to show that it had been channelling inquiries back and forth between countries. It was recognized that committee programmes ambitiously undertaken at annual conferences tended to founder because of the inability of key members, especially the co-chairmen, to devote sufficient time. Considerable attention was given to the need for computer auditing expertise on a world-wide basis, and it was agreed that a computer auditing section would be set up under the accounting and auditing committee. The personnel and training committee recommended that MML partnerships be provided to give career opportunities for deserving young men and to attract them to overseas service. An innovation adopted was the division of the participants into small groups to discuss the points raised by speakers and contributors of papers, after which the results of the discussion groups were aired in plenary session. The meeting was attended by eighty-two partners (thirty-two from the UK), many with their wives, representing twenty-two firms from twenty-one countries.

The sixth international meeting was held in Germany in September 1971. Seventy-seven partners and forty-three wives attended, representing twenty-eight firms from twenty-four countries. There seemed to be a feeling of greater accomplishment on the part of the technical committees. The previously postponed MML training programme was presented and the draft of the first section of an MML audit manual was reviewed. The tax committee completed a manual on procedures for the processing of inquiries to be circulated among tax liaison men, and proposed preparation of the manual later published as *A guide to the Taxation and Related Problems of Companies Expanding Abroad.*

The seventh international meeting held in Melbourne, Australia, in October 1972, had a top client official, Mr Gene Burns, vice-president finance of CPC International Inc, as a guest speaker. Because of the relatively smaller size of this meeting, there were no meetings of the technical committees. There was some disappointment expressed at this, and it was felt to have inhibited their progress. The policy committee announced the broadening of the underwriting firms group with the addition of Australia and Holland. Also, there was further discussion about the necessity of MML providing some sort of guidance and instruction on computer auditing, with some critical comment on the limited action taken to date. Finally, to the consternation of some of the more conservative members, the subject of public relations, press releases and the like, was discussed.

The eighth international meeting was held in Mexico City in October 1973, with eighty-nine partners (eighty-five from countries other than Mexico) and fifty-five wives attending—by far the broadest representation, thirty-eight countries and thirty firms, in the history of these meetings. One day was devoted to a discussion of currency problems. No answer or common approach was found, but there was considerable interest in the guest speaker on the subject, Dr Redvers Opie, who had been a member of the original UK delegation to the Bretton Woods conference. There was a noticeable desire among all firms represented to become more and more involved in the day-to-day running of MML. This showed itself in the keen interest in reorganization proposals. There was also a substantial commitment to quality control reviews. On communications, there were several instances where discussion groups called for regular, possibly quarterly, publications to all member firms advising of actions of the New York and London administrations and other matters which had involved the MML group. This advice was later implemented in part.

The ninth annual meeting was held in Ireland in September 1974, and was notable for a wide-ranging and lucid account of the philosophy, genesis and development of MML by James Halsey, one of the US partners most closely involved in MML work. The 1975 conference, in Amsterdam, was probably the most successful and certainly the most expensive to date, with 114 partners and ninety-three wives, plus Dutch partners. There were two guest speakers, one a senior executive of Philips talking about the problems facing a multi-national company, with interesting parallels for MML, and the second, Professor Drs van 't Klooster on computer auditing and computer frauds. The three MML partners reported, and there was discussion of client and practice development and, most important, of the proposed 'quality control' document to be prepared world-wide by each of the member firms. It was generally agreed that although MML was by its very constitution not entitled to dictate to its members, nevertheless it could give guidance and advice, and the quality review teams were entitled to look at all facets of a firm's organization in order to evaluate the general health of MML as a whole.

Here we have a hint of the fact that a federation like MML, however autonomous its units, does need a degree of commonality and co-ordination if it is to work. Accordingly, in 1974 there came into being a new operational structure for MML, which is set out diagrammatically in the chart at the end of this chapter. In this structure, except for certain fundamental matters reserved to the five principal firms (in which, incidentally, TMcL has four votes out of fifteen), the Board of Management is responsible for all the affairs of MML and all the decisions in its administration, including the approval of revenue budgets and the admission of new member firms. The Board of Management has fourteen members, nine from the founding firms, and decisions are by a simple majority, which must, however, include five of the nine; TMcL has two representatives on the Board of Management. The day-to-day administration of MML is, however, handled by a western and an eastern executive, as illustrated in the chart on page 146.

The Board of Management has an independent chairman who does not have a vote but is readily responsible for the development of MML. The first chairman of the Board of Management was LeRoy Layton, then recently retired as senior partner of Main Lafrentz. A past president of the AICPA and indubitably a leader in the world-wide profession of accountancy, Lee Layton was one of the central figures in the creation and progress of MML, so it was fitting that he should become the first chairman of the new MML set-up.

In the year which ended 31 March 1966, the first year for which financial statements were prepared for MML and, indeed, the first official year of its operations, the Eastern Hemisphere reported total fees on referred work of only about $45,000. For 1976 the figure is over $5,000,000.

During the first year of operation, work which had been done by the predecessor firms was continued but none of it represented any major new commitment by a multi-national client. The first breakthrough came in 1967, when the Hewlett Packard Company of the United States entrusted most of their overseas audit work to MML for the year then ended. This engagement immediately involved almost all the then existing European offices and several in Latin America. Shortly after, the Grand Metropolitan group of the United Kingdom began expanding its hotel operations into Europe. The MML European offices were entrusted with this work, and other offices of MML have since undertaken single or continuing engagements for this client as far afield as Japan. Other smaller United States clients began placing more and more of their overseas work with MML in the period from 1967 to 1969—Eastern Air Devices, Keewanee/Harshaw, Selas Corporation of America, and the Amiro subsidiaries of Triangle Industries. UK clients which figured in the expansion of MML during its early years were the Oddeninos Group, the John Laing Group, Common Bros, Stenhouse, and Tube Investments, as well as many one-off investigations.

As MML acquired experience and proved its competence,

the United States firm moved positively towards transfer of its major client work into MML and many MML offices now include among their clients Pfizer and CPC International.

As recently as the year ended March 1971, the major proportion of MML volume originated in the United States — in that year almost 80%. In 1972 this proportion was roughly 70%, in 1973 about 65%, and in 1974 the percentage of the United States work again decreased to 54% although the total volume of referred work from the United States continues to increase year by year.

The significance of this is not only the increase in the United Kingdom referred work but also the increase in referrals among other members of the MML group. This indicates that MML is now becoming a real multi-national partnership with all offices referring work to one another rather than the US-supported network that it was at the outset. There have been significant referrals among the countries comprising the European Economic Community, and between Latin-American countries, as well as increased activity for non-US companies in the United States. The quarterly meetings of partners from all over Europe, held primarily to improve communications, have also helped to generate referrals between European firms.

With this growth, both in absolute terms and in non-US business, it is no wonder that in his 1974 survey of MML, Halsey was able to say with some confidence that 'MML no longer has the distinction of being the largest unknown accounting firm in the world', and Morrison in the same year could say that MML, having been described by some as 'ghosting' around the international scene, was now assuming a remarkably material form for a 'ghost'.

As with the partners of TMcL, partners in MML firms participate fully in the work of the professional bodies of their countries, many having risen to the highest offices in these bodies.

ORGANIZATION OF McLINTOCK MAIN LAFRENTZ-INTERNATIONAL

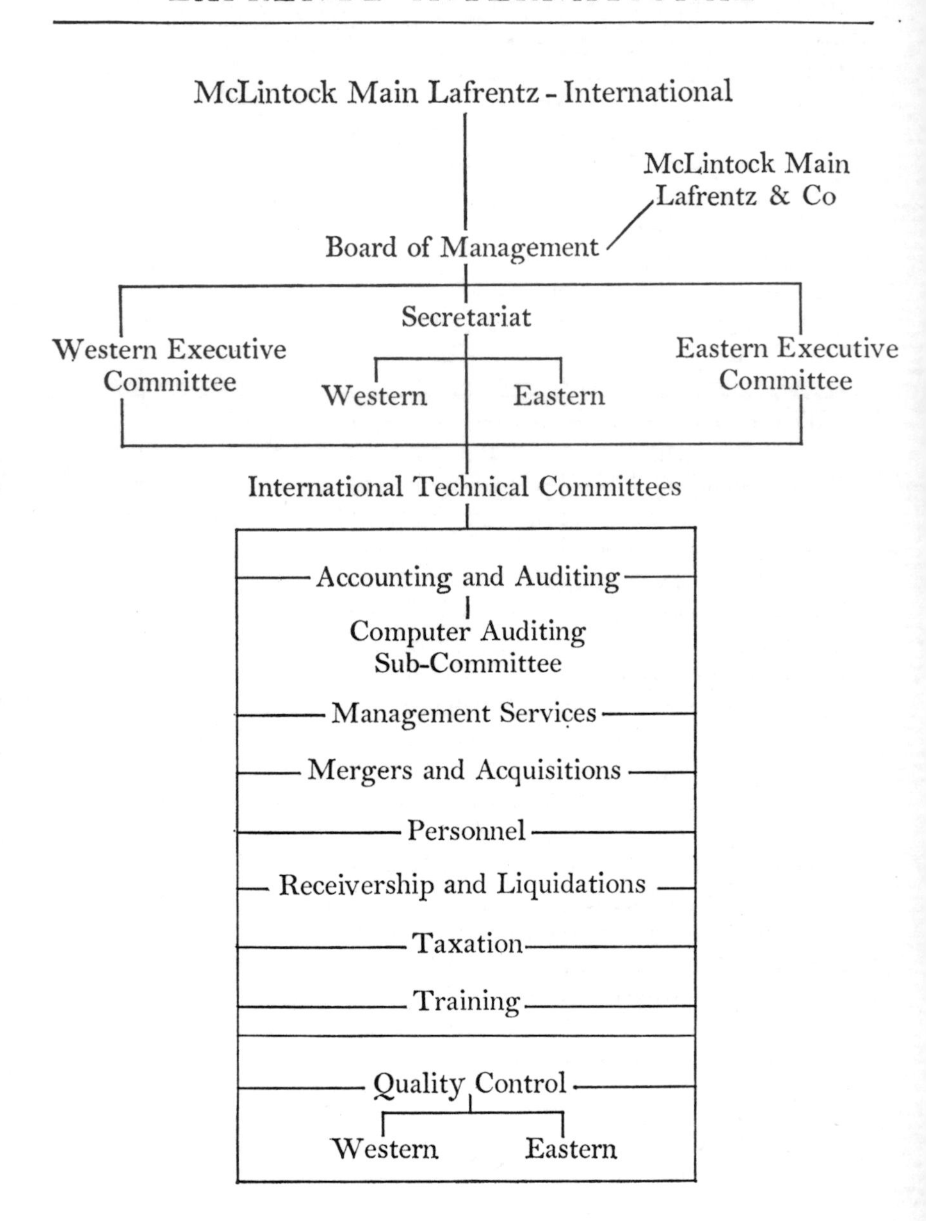

Conclusion

WE HAVE seen how over a century Thomson McLintock & Co has grown and organized itself, in the earlier period in response to the ambitions and personalities of certain dominant figures who were usually but not always members of the founding family, and later in response to the business pressures and challenges of the post-war period. Inevitably the traditions of the firm and the outlook of the partners in it have inter-reacted with the competitive environment, both within the UK and internationally, to produce a system of government and shape of organization which TMcL is almost certainly the largest firm in the profession to evolve. Clear contrasts have been drawn with both the pace and the style of development of other accountancy firms, as they responded to what were basically the same set of business challenges, notably the internationalization of big business, particularly US big business in the form of the US multinational corporations.

The rate of change and growth at Thomson McLintock & Co has been particularly marked in the ten to twelve years preceding its centenary, as the firm was more or less forced to take a fresh look at itself and re-assess the possibilities, partly as a conscious thought-out policy of development, and partly in an opportunist fashion as particular situations and chances arose. The result has been a rather complex but nevertheless flexible structure whose overwhelmingly most important virtue is that it seeks to tailor the system to the people, and not vice versa. Almost all organizations move, whether gradually or by sudden jumps and reversals, between ideas of centralization and decentralization; but McLintocks has firmly elected to take a clear position at one end of the spectrum, that of the decentralized non-authoritarian federation.

Now established as a conscious philosophy of life—one might even venture to call it a political philosophy, since politics is, after all, the art of government—this position nevertheless was arrived at as much out of necessity as of thought, when it was realized that the only way to gain the size and geographical spread needed to compete in the big league of accountancy firms was to link with established and usually flourishing firms in the various centres of activity who were certainly not going to surrender their individuality and freedoms to some anonymous big brother corporation. In that sense, McLintocks has consciously if inevitably sought to preserve much of the spirit of a traditional organization of professional men, rather than try to approximate as far as possible, as some other accountancy firms have done, to the organizational structure and management philosophy of the trading and manufacturing organizations which are their major clients.

The general view at TMcL is that after this hectic bout of activity lasting, roughly, from 1965 to 1975, a period of relative calm and consolidation is probably called for—perhaps in tune with the more contemplative mood engendered by reaching the age of 100. But business cannot stand still. It is quite possible that in between the writing of these words and their publication further changes may take place; what is quite certain is that further changes will take place before too long. That is the nature of the business environment. So it is not inappropriate at this point to take stock of what type of change may be foreseen, and what type of problem and challenge may influence the decisions of the partners of Thomson McLintock & Co in the foreseeable future (whatever that may be, in these uncertain times). Such 'guesstimates' about the future must inevitably be hedged with caution; but without them one cannot achieve a fully rounded picture of the firm. A person's hopes and fears about the future are as much part of his make-up as his history of past mistakes and successes; so it is also with organizations, especially ones which, like Thomson McLintock & Co, are now deeply involved with the fortunes of the world economy rather than just with the limited parish of England and Scotland (which is not to say, incidentally, that being the largest native Scottish firm of accountants, in a part of Great Britain with great economic prospects thanks to North Sea oil, may not turn out to be the strongest single card in the TMcL pack).

In general terms, a firm in the position of TMcL must have its eyes and ears open for one or more of the following types of expansion opportunity. One is a merger with another national firm, in the interests of size and competitiveness with the largest in the business; at this stage it is impossible to know for sure or for good where the logic of its recent expansion may eventually take the firm, although it seems doubtful whether it could ever contemplate a link with a firm which had overseas connections of any substance, because of McLintocks' tie with Main Lafrentz of the USA and Thorne Riddell of Canada. Secondly, it might look closely at a firm whose main recommendation was its list of clients. Thirdly, it might repeat what it has done in the past, and form further links with good local firms, to 'fill in' its national coverage.

In broad terms, as we have seen, this national coverage is now regarded as more or less complete, especially in Scotland. But in England a simple glance at the map might suggest that the East Coast and East Anglia is not exactly rich in TMcL personnel. Similarly, the Exeter office operated from Bristol was to some extent an alternative to finding a local firm to take under the TMcL wing, and it is therefore quite possible that sooner or later, as has happened in so many cities of the UK, a TMcL office may come first and only later be absorbed into a local firm that joins the McLintock federation. Again, Cardiff is at the time of writing a small office, and one may ask, as TMcL men themselves do, what will be the right direction to take in Wales. Moreover, as already narrated, it was once proposed to carry out a merger in Sheffield, rather than simply have an office, and it would be surprising if this matter were not periodically reviewed in the light of changing circumstances.

Internationally, this geographical view of TMcL's position has inevitably raised questions about the penetration of MML into Africa, into the oil-rich areas of the Middle East and, increasingly, into growth regions such as Brazil. A lot of intensive effort has gone into establishing representation in these areas of the world. But at least as important, if not more so in terms of the effort needed to meet the problem, was the clear requirement for a better coverage of Europe. This was a problem that fell squarely within the bailiwick of McLintocks of the UK, it being responsible through the executive committee for the Eastern Hemisphere operations of MML. It was not so much a problem of standards, although it is fair to say that quality control and training have been and are the two most urgent on-going activities.

Rather, it was a question of identifying and linking with firms throughout Europe which combine high standards of work with the will and ability to be expansionist-minded. Expansion was really the key, both in the UK and abroad. For just as in the UK the main disadvantage of having a small branch office in a given city is that it is not really a good basis for expansion; so in Europe attitudes to expansion were not necessarily similar from country to country or from firm to firm. In any case, the future pattern of accountancy across Europe is as yet far from clear. Both the activities of the US multi-nationals and the progress of the European Economic Community would suggest more and larger trans-European groupings than have so far emerged. So far, nationalist pressures have proved as strong as internationalist, and it is in this area, and with its own particular style and philosophy of organization, that TMcL may have the key to how pan-European groupings may arise in greater numbers and with greater cohesion. It is an area where the competitive situation against the big eight accountancy firms is not the same as elsewhere, and where MML has already established a pattern of constructive and successful meetings between personnel from various European MML affiliates. In short, Europe will be a particularly fascinating area to watch, both in terms of the development of accountancy in general, and in terms of TMcL's own specific progress in it. Running through all the international business will also be the common thread of the problem of currency translation.

Nearer home, the main costs that are shared by all the regional firms of the TMcL confederacy are those to do with training, and those to do with MML—the losses or, if you prefer the description, the development costs incurred in setting up the international organization. But there is within the firm a current of opinion that believes that greater pooling of resources is sooner or later inevitable, whatever may be the right and natural system at this moment. Clearly, pooling of profits would be the greatest single expression of the consolidation of TMcL's finances. Some may see pooling of profits as striking at the very heart of the federal idea; some may see it as a nettle to be grasped in time; some may see it as the shape of things to come, but not, so to speak, 'in my lifetime'. It is a characteristic virtue of Thomson McLintock & Co that diverse attitudes on this and other questions can co-exist and be stated without embarrassment, as part of the open style of self-government that is the firm's hallmark.

Similarly, having got itself out of the trap of London partners being more equal than other partners, the question of the pooling of the human resources of the firm, as a means of their rational allocation, seems an obvious question that will occupy the minds of the partners. There is, of course, already a degree of mobility between offices, as for example the three partners that went from London to Manchester, and the partner from the north-east and the partner from Belfast that went to London; only time will show how far this process can or should be taken. One may also suppose that interchange of people within MML may increase over time, and even speculate whether the requirements of inflation accounting, now such an issue in the United Kingdom, may bring more rather than less diversity between the accountancy practices of various countries, so necessitating more interchange of information and people.

Clearly, therefore, for this and for many other reasons, the business of communications within Thomson McLintock & Co and within MML is going to assume more and more importance, both as a result of size and growth, and as a result of the system of self-government that the two interconnecting organizations have chosen for themselves; for if communications begin to break down, then the whole idea of consent and consensus as the means of self-control will begin to break down too. That is why such a large part of many people's time in TMcL is inevitably spent in travelling to meetings and conferences, and why steps to formalize the system of internal communication have already been taken. It will be a formidable enough task to ensure good communications among the 100 or more UK partners, let alone the 1,500 or more employees of TMcL, and it is a task that must be tackled with full realization of its importance.

But in facing the future and in meeting those challenges which can be foreseen, as well as those which cannot, the firm can draw upon a range of strengths that are rooted in its history and in its methods. Here really lies the justification for relating that history; for however firmly a practical businessman or professional man may fix his eye on the immediate horizon, the fact is that few business situations are fully explicable without reference to their history, and few groups of people are fully explicable in terms of what they do and why, without reference to *their* history.

So a centenary history of TMcL is no mere antiquarian exercise. The motto 'know thyself' applies to firms as well as to individuals, and one does not, like Socrates who originally said it, have to stand stock still for hours or days on end in order to 'know thyself'. It is all part and parcel of the on-going business of running the organization and planning for the future. McLintocks' hundred-year history has been eventful, peopled with men of high professional standing and unusual force of personality, and marked by policies and reactions to changing circumstances that were by no means stereotyped, but showed an unusual degree of friendliness and respect for fellow human beings. It is more than a pious wish, and more than idle speculation, to hope that these same qualities may see the firm through many more decades to come.

FULL LIST OF TMcL PARTNERS
1877–1977
(listed by office of residence)

ABERDEEN

Steven Leslie Henderson*	1968–
John McBain	1968–
Alan Gordon McBain	1968–
John Leslie Athol Munro	1971–
Alan David John Amoore	1976–

(all, with the exception of ADJ Amoore, were previously partners in G & J McBain which merged with TMcL Aberdeen on 1 April 1971)

BIRMINGHAM

Holwell Hely Hutchinson Walshe*(1)	1921–1946	
Ralph Edward Herington*(2)	1936–1961	
Henry Maurice Pritchard*(3)	1949–1976	
Alan Aitken Davies	1949–	
Harold Burgess Thomas Wilde	1963–1970	ex Aston Wilde & Co
Victor Frank Stedeford	1963–1970	ex Aston Wilde & Co
William Parker	1963–1973	ex Aston Wilde & Co
John Constantine*(4)	1964–	
Richard Edward Gordon†	1968–1969	
Nigel Frederick Luckett	1970–	
Alexander Lewis Weir	1970–	
John Nicholas Dearn Pritchard	1975–	
Stephen Geoffrey Mills	1975–	
Norman Richard Gillhespy	1975–	

* senior partners (1) 1921–1946 (2) 1946–1961 (3) 1961–1976 (4) 1976–

† see also list of partners in Leicester

DUNDEE

Andrew Whamond Mudie*	1973–
Donald Blane Grant	1973–
John Reid Watson	1973–
Ronald William Gibson	1973–
Gordon Stuart Lowden	1973–
David Laing Macpherson	1973–
Ian George Stevenson	1973–
Roger Thomas Leslie	1975–

(all eight were previously partners in Moody Stuart & Robertson which merged with TMcL Dundee on 1 April 1975)

GLASGOW/EDINBURGH

Thomson McLintock*(1)	1877–1920
William McLintock† (Sir William McLintock)	1901–1914
Thomson Liddell McLintock*(2)	1901–1940
William Gilmour	1901–1919
John Duncan*(3)	1916–1960
William Anderson	1920–1935
Harold Ernest Borland	1920–1954
John Morison† (Sir John Morison)	1920–1926
James Thompson Dowling*(4)	1931–1969
Thomas Chalmers Currie	1931–1965
John Haig Haddow	1931–1961
Richard Thomson Young	1941–1971
John Alexander Gardner Kerr	1946–1971
Donald Angus Robertson	1946–1964
John Waldie*(5)	1946–1974
Thomson Ian McLintock	1949–1965
David Maitland Duncan	1952–1961
John Neill Anderson	1958–
John Lister Kirkpatrick*(6)	1958–
John Dewar Tebb	1961–1966
Matthew David McPhail	1961–
John Cumming Craig	1965–
Robert Westwater Speirs	1966–

GLASGOW/EDINBURGH (continued)

William Charles Carnegie Morrison*(7)	1966–
George David Caldwell	1966–
Blair Smith	1966–
Peter Leslie Stewart	1968–
Thomas Stewart McDougall	1971–
Thomas Scott Rutherford	1971–
Gordon Nicoll Simpson	1971–
William Drysdale	1972–
June Priscilla Brown	1973–
Ian Scott Murdoch	1973–
George Morris Gibb	1974–
Archibald Sinclair Hunter	1974–
James Young Miller	1974–
John Hugh Alexander Campbell Crawford	‡1975–1976
William John Muir Alexander	‡1975–
Hugh McMichael	‡1975–
Gordon Gillies Ruffle	‡1975–
Maurice Coghill Murphy	‡1975–
Thomas Cowan Steven	‡1975–
George Fraser Davidson	‡1975–
William Ronald Barnetson	‡1975–
David Younger Johnston	‡1975–
David Mackay Nicolson	‡1975–
Bryan John Rankin	‡1975–

* senior partners (1) 1877–1920 (2) 1920–1940 (3) 1940–1960 (4) 1960–1969 (5) 1969–1974 (6) 1974– (7) 1974–

† see also list of partners in London

‡ year of joining TMcL from Robertson & Maxtone Graham

INVERNESS AND THURSO

Henry Dickson Park Brown*	1975–
Peter Cullen	1975–
Forbes Ritchie Philip	1975–
James Craighead Pringle	1975–
James Ian Brough	1975–
Andrew Raymond Duncan	1975–

Robert Stewart Palombo	1976–

(all seven are partners in Frame Kennedy & Forrest)

LEICESTER

Richard Edward Gordon†	1965–1969
Alastair William Gray	1970–
John Hampton Golcher*	1974–
Nigel Henry Parkinson	1974–
Arthur Stanley Price	1974–
Michael Aubrey Chamberlain	1974–
Alexander Douglas Blount	1974–
Michael John Linnett	1974–
John Roward Newton Lowe	1974–

(all except RE Gordon and AW Gray were previously partners in Baker Bros Halford & Co which merged with TMcL on 1 January 1974)

† see also list of partners in Birmingham

LISBON

Alasdair James Mackintosh	1973–

LONDON

William McLintock*(1) (Sir William McLintock)	1914–1947
Charles Henry McLintock	1914–1918 1934–1947
James Charteris Burleigh*(2)	1920–1951
John Morison*(3) (Sir John Morison)	1926–1958
Thomas Lister*(4)	1931–1967
Duncan McKellar	1931–1967
Thomson McLintock (jnr)	1934–1941
Lionel Harold Harvey Lowe (Sir Lionel Lowe)	1935–1946
John Kissane	1935–1941
John Kennedy Cockburn Millar	1936–1946
Robert Simpson	1937–1967

LONDON (continued)

Gerald Bradley*(5)	1946–1968	
Leslie Robert Bell	1946–1972	
William Kenneth MacLeod Slimmings*(6) (Sir William Slimmings)	1946–	
Ernest Ferguson Milne	1948–	
James Travers Hamilton Macnair	1953–	
Robert Mackenzie Morison	1954–	
Charles Alan McLintock	1954–	
Clifford John Smith	1959–1974	
Arthur Murray Campbell Morison	1961–	
Ian Glendinning Watt	1963–	
George Cecil Bannerman Kellagher	1964–	
John Dashwood St Clair Harrison	1967–	
Frank Alexander Harding	1967–	
Martin Gardiner Adamson	1967–	
Dennis Anthony Thornley	1968–	ex Martin Farlow & Co
Francis George Lyon	1968–	
Gordon McAllister	1969–	
Michael Geoffrey Minton Haines	1969–	
Sven Leslie Cecil Tester	1969–	
Christopher John Nash Williams	1970–	
Michael Gibson Crabtree	1970–	
Peter David Bailey	1970–	
Mary Anora Yale	1971–	
Miles Crispin Dean Roberts	1972–	
Alpin Findanus MacGregor	1972–	
William Lindop Hall†	1973–	
Nigel William Morrison May‡	1974–	
David Arthur	1975–	
William List	1975–	
Alexander George Bogie	1975–	
George Purves McNaught	1976–	

* senior partners (1) 1914–1947 (2) 1947–1954 (3) 1954–1958 (4) 1958–1967 (5) 1967–1968 (6) 1968–

† see also list of partners in the North East

‡ see also list of partners in Northern Ireland

NORTH EAST

George Moncur Reid	1963–
Arnold Cecil Dixon*(1)	1966–1972
George Dobie Weir	1966–1972
Alan Whittaker*(2)	1966–
John Norris	1966–
Dominic Thomas Scarre Rutter	1966–
William Lindop Hall†	1966–1973
Denis Anthony Courtney	1966–
John Lewis Hinkley	1974–
Roger Murray Griffiths	1975–

(all except GM Reid, JL Hinkley and RM Griffiths were previously partners in Squance & Co which merged with TMcL on 1 December 1966)

* senior partners (1) 1966–1972 (2) 1972–
† see also list of partners in London

NORTH WEST

Robert Paterson*(1)	1930–1933	
Thomas Cochrane Guthrie*(2)	1933–1958	
James Stephen Harrower	1947–1953	
James Alexander Brown*(3)	1953–1975	
John Douglas Miller	1958–1974	
William McLaughlin*(4)	1965–	
Marmaduke Bell	1966–1971	ex Sir Charles H Wilson & Co
John Hutchings Rhodes	1966–	ex Sir Charles H Wilson & Co
Barry Gordon Drew	1968–	
Ninian Aitken Watt	1970–	
David Jeremy Illingworth	1976–	

* senior partners (1) 1930–1933 (2) 1933–1958 (3) 1958–1975 (4) 1975–

NORTHERN IRELAND

Nigel William Morrison May*(1)†	1970–1974
Peter Jefferson Artt*(2)	1970–
David Alvin Bradshaw	1975–

(NWM May and PJ Artt were previously partners in May & Co which merged with TMcL on 1 April 1970)

* senior partners (1) 1970–1974 (2) 1974–
† see also list of partners in London

SOUTH WEST

Donald James Ironside*(1)	1969–
Charles Herbert Maggs	1969–1970
Philip Hugh Dyer	1969–
David Michael Parkes*(2)	1969–
Henry Gerard Mather Leighton	1969–1970
Allan Anderson Gillon	1969–1971
Gerald James King	1969–
Patricia Lewis	1969–
David William Robert Johnstone	1969–
Robert Stanley Porter	1969–1969 (December)
Melville James Dron	1972–
Gerald Arthur Sturtridge	1974–
Gregory Keith Cairns	1974–
Alfred Edward Hill	1974–

(all except MJ Dron, GA Sturtridge, GK Cairns and AE Hill were partners in Grace Ryland & Co which merged with TMcL on 1 January 1969)

* senior partners (1) 1969–1974 (2) 1974–

Certain of the above held, or hold, partnerships in TMcL offices in which they were, or are, not resident. For the sake of simplicity mention is not made of these.

* senior partner

NUMBERS OF PARTNERS AND STAFF IN THE UNITED KINGDOM

	Partners	*Staff*
Aberdeen	5	45
Birmingham	7	115
Dundee	8	33
Edinburgh	12	147
Glasgow	16	186
Inverness & Thurso	7	53
Leicester	8	97
London	28	520
North East – Newcastle	5	45
Darlington	2	34
North West – Manchester	3	51
Leeds	2	34
Liverpool	–	5
Sheffield	–	10
Northern Ireland – Belfast	2	19
South West – Bristol	9	105
Cardiff	–	1
Exeter	1	5
	115	1,514

THOMSON McLINTOCK GROWTH TREE

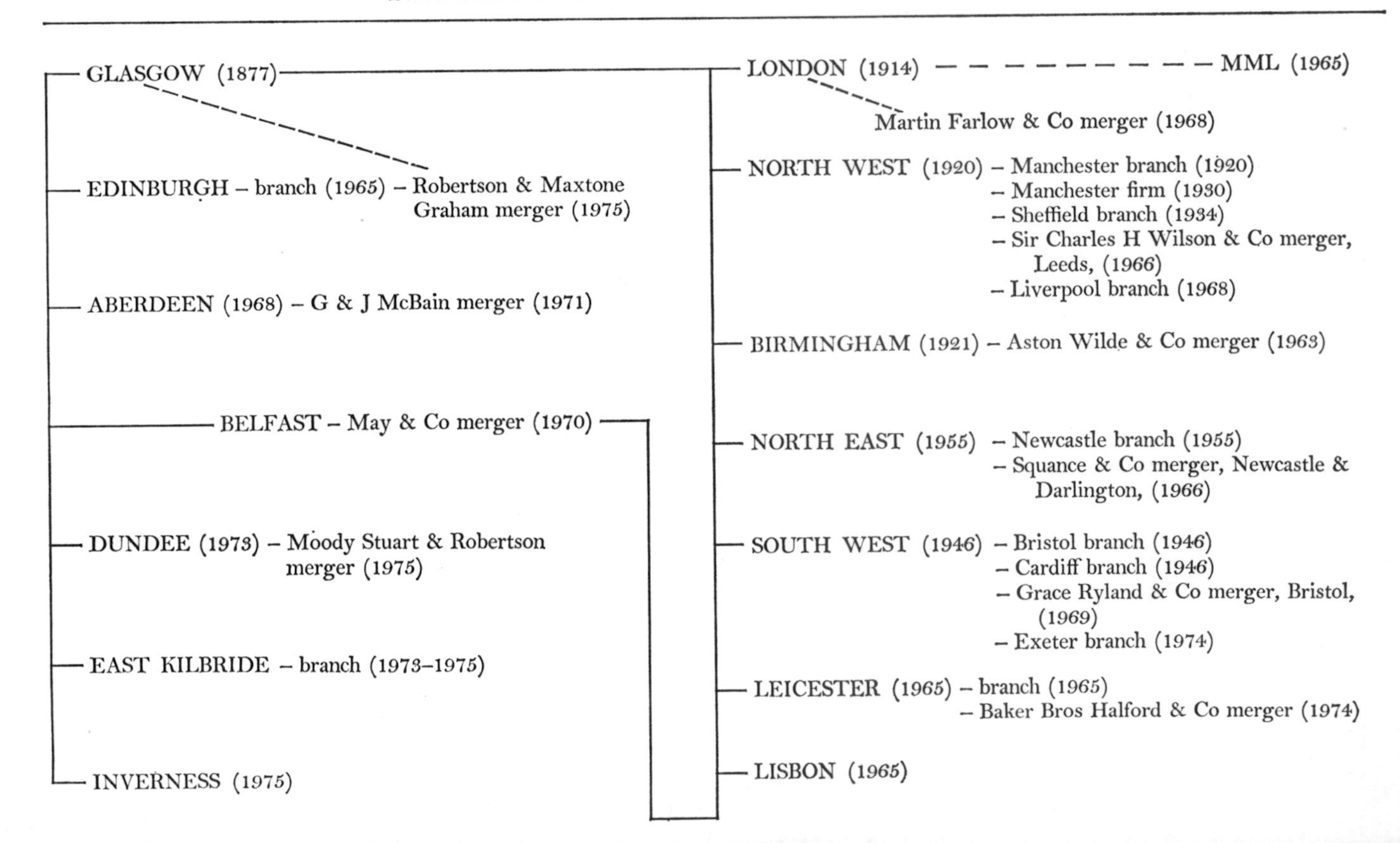

NATIONAL FIRMS FORMING THE McLINTOCK MAIN LAFRENTZ & CO GROUP

ARGENTINA:	Pickenhayn y Asociados
AUSTRALIA:	Hancock & Offner
AUSTRIA:	Austria Wirtschaftspruefungs AG
BAHAMAS:	Thorne Riddell & Co
BARBADOS:	Thorne Riddell & Co
BELGIUM:	Pelser, Hamelberg, Van Til & Co
BERMUDA:	Rawlinson, Hunter, Butterfield & Co
BRAZIL:	Walter Heuer Auditores Independentes
CANADA:	Thorne Riddell & Co
CAYMAN ISLANDS:	Rawlinson, Hunter, Butterfield & Co
CHANNEL ISLANDS:	Reads & Co
CHILE:	Wulf, Valdivieso, Salas y Cia Ltda
COLOMBIA:	Juan Jose Amezquita & Co
COSTA RICA:	Despacho Lic Fernando Murillo Marchini & Asociados
DENMARK:	Revisionsfirmaet Mortensen & Beierholm
FINLAND:	Borje Forsstrom & Co Revisionsbyra
FRANCE:	Fiduciaire Continentale
GERMANY:	Fides Treuhandgesellschaft Karoli Wirtschaftspruefung GmbH
GREECE:	HD Kontos & Company
HOLLAND:	Pelser, Hamelberg, Van Til & Co
HONDURAS:	Fortin, Lagos y Asociados
HONG KONG:	John BP Byrne & Co
INDIA:	SB Billimoria & Co
INDONESIA:	PT SGV-Utomo Drs Utomo, Mulia & Co
IRAN:	Amin & Co

IRELAND:	Cooper Magennis
ITALY:	Revisori Internazionali Associati SpA
JAPAN:	Sanwa Tokyo Marunouchi & Co
KENYA:	Kassim-Lakha Abdulla & Co
KUWAIT:	Fauzi F Saba & Associates
LEBANON:	Fauzi F Saba & Associates
MALAYSIA:	SGV-Kassim Chan Sdn Bhd Kassim, Chan & Co
MEXICO:	Rodolfo Hernandez y Asociados, SC
NEW ZEALAND:	Morris, Pattrick & Co
NIGERIA:	ZO Ososanya & Co
NORWAY:	Mohn's Revisjonsbyra
PANAMA:	Buron y Asociados
PAPUA NEW GUINEA:	Hancock & Offner
PERU:	Alonso, Castro y Asociados
PHILIPPINES:	SyCip, Gorres, Velayo & Co
PORTUGAL:	Thomson McLintock & Co
PUERTO RICO:	Machargo Del Rio, Ramon & Associates
SAUDI-ARABIA:	Fauzi F Saba & Associate
SINGAPORE:	SGV-Goh Tan Pte Ltd Goh, Tan & Co
SOUTH AFRICA:	Alex Aiken & Carter
SOUTH KOREA:	Ahn, Kwon & Co
SPAIN:	LC Hopewell
SWAZILAND:	Alex Aiken & Carter
SWEDEN:	Karlgrens Revisionsbyra Aktiebolag
SWITZERLAND:	Societe de Controle Fiduciaire SA International Trust Ltd
TAIWAN:	SGV-Soong & Co TN Soong & Co
THAILAND:	SGV-Na Thalang & Co Ltd Y Na Thalang & Co
UNITED ARAB EMIRATES:	Fauzi F Saba & Associates
UNITED KINGDOM:	Thomson McLintock & Co
UNITED STATES OF AMERICA:	Main Lafrentz & Co
URUGUAY:	TEA Consultores Asociados
VENEZUELA:	Cimarro & Asociados

(The very few localities in which McLintock Main Lafrentz is represented by other British national firms are not included above)